Steven Lawson's hallmark is passio
into a contagious enthusiasm for o
all the preachers in church history Dr Lawson has read
perhaps none has stirred him more than John Knox. In these
pages he celebrates the five hundredth anniversary of the Scottish
Reformer's birth by a vivid retelling of the story of his life and
ministry and by applying some of the most important lessons of
his remarkable life and ministry. Take a deep breath as you turn
the first page; this story may leave you breathless; but you will
almost certainly feel spiritually fitter by the end!

Sinclair B Ferguson,
Chancellor's Professor of Systematic Theology, Reformed Theological
Seminary, Jackson, Mississippi

Steven Lawson writes with characteristic verve and passion and
captures the aroma of Christ in the lives of his subjects. He has
done this with unusual clarity and conviction with the figure
of John Knox. Knox, in spite of his detractors, remains one of
the pivotal figures in the Reformation of the church in Europe,
England and most especially Scotland. But it is as a preacher and
leader that he is most remembered. Dr Lawson helps us catch the
vision and passion of this 'lion' in the pulpit. In his hands Knox
lives and has much to teach the church in our generation.

Liam Goligher,
Senior Minister, Tenth Presbyterian Church, Philadelphia, Pennsylvania

John Knox preached with such courage that we might well say
the Spirit of Christ gave him a face harder than flint (Ezek. 3:8-9).
Steven Lawson, himself a bold preacher, has given us a biography
of Knox that inspires similar courage. In this day of jellyfish, may
God use this book to raise up more Christians like Knox!

Joel R. Beeke,
President
Puritan Reformed Theological Seminary, Grand Rapids, Michigan

This is a little gem of a book. Steven Lawson has written a timely biography of John Knox, the father of the Scottish Reformation. The twentieth century saw Knox's reputation attacked from many quarters. Authors as diverse as Hugh McDiarmid, Edwin Muir and Neil Oliver, were critical of Knox for his uncompromising outlook. Knox's reputation has been restored in more recent times by the sympathetic and perceptive biography by Rosalind K. Marshall, and Lawson's work continues this movement of bringing Knox and his contribution into renewed serious consideration. Lawson outlines Knox's contribution in a clear, lucid style, giving the narrative an engaging manner. What is particularly noteworthy is the way Lawson is able to introduce significant aspects of Knox's thinking on various issues in an easy to absorb elegance. The book is well researched and, though written in an easy popular style, it contains significant detail which will satisfy the reader who wishes to understand Knox's life and thought. Lawson is especially strong in highlighting Martyn Lloyd-Jones' estimate of Knox as the true 'first of the Puritans, even more than Calvin.' This is an excellent production and I thoroughly recommend it both to the general reader and to the student who is looking for an introduction to Knox's life and faith.

Bruce Ritchie,
Lecturer in Church History,
Highland Theological College, Dingwall, Scotland

In the providence of God, and especially since the Reformation, the Scottish people have played a remarkable role in the advance of the Gospel. And at the heart of the Reformation, a key turning-point in the history of this Celtic people, is the life and ministry of the subject of these pages, John Knox. In the brief compass of this book, Steven Lawson has captured the essence and main contours of Knox's vital ministry—no easy task. Read and ponder, and then pray that God would raise up again such thunderers of the Bible as Knox—yes, in Scotland, and to the ends of the earth.

Michael A.G. Haykin,
Professor of Church History & Biblical Spirituality,
The Southern Baptist Theological Seminary, Louisville, Kentucky

It was 'fearless faith' that enabled a man from an unlikely backdrop to transform a Church and a nation. When John Knox came on the scene in the mid 16th century darkness, ignorance and corruption prevailed in Scotland. Satan had, through subtlety, deprived the Church of the spiritual weapons potent to destroy the kingdom of darkness. Knox, emboldened by a vision of the majesty of God and full of zeal for the glory of Christ, used the mighty weapon of the preached Word to remake the Church and the nation. He succeeded under God to see a Church founded on God's Word and cleansed by God's Spirit. Steven Lawson here relates the story with a similar passion to have that same preached Word restore the Church in our day. May many catch that vision as a result!

John J. Murray (1935–2020),
Author of *John Knox: A Bitesize Biography,*
Minister of the Free Church of Scotland (Continuing), Glasgow

Readers of Stephen Lawson's biography will gain an understanding of why Knox has retained his position in the history of the Scottish Church down through the generations. This is a popular history, characterized by passion, quoting throughout the words of Knox himself, and written in the tradition of Knox's own *History of the Reformation of Religion in Scotland.*

John R. McIntosh,
Professor of Church History and Church Principles,
Edinburgh Theological Seminary, Edinburgh, Scotland

Dr Steven Lawson is exactly the church history writer the church needs today. John Knox is exactly the church history figure the church needs today. And here we have them both together. Read this book, and pray for a measure of the passion for the gospel you will read about in these pages.

Stephen J. Nichols,
President, Reformation Bible College,
CAO, Ligonier Ministries, Sanford, Florida

Steven Lawson has written an excellent popular introduction to the life and achievements of John Knox. Indeed one can sense the fire of Knox's own faith burning in these pages. Outside of his native Scotland, Knox has been overshadowed by other giants of the Reformation, such as Luther, Zwingli, and Calvin. I trust, however, that this biography will bring Knox to life for a new generation of readers, enabling them to appreciate the man's true greatness, and his eminent services to the Reformation of the 16th century.

Nick Needham,
Lecturer in Church History,
Highland Theological College, Dingwall, Scotland

JOHN KNOX

Fearless Faith

STEVEN J. LAWSON

CHRISTIAN
FOCUS

Dr. Steven J. Lawson is President and founder of OnePassion Ministries in Dallas, Texas. He is also a Teaching Fellow for Ligonier Ministries and Professor of Preaching at The Master's Seminary, Sun Valley, California. In addition, Dr. Lawson is Professor in Residence for Truth Remains. He is the author of over twenty books and speaks at conferences around the world. He and his wife, Anne, have four children.

Copyright © Steven J. Lawson 2014

paperback ISBN 978-1-78191-539-4
epub ISBN 978-1-78191-544-8
Mobi ISBN 978-1-78191-549-3

10 9 8 7 6 5 4 3 2 1

First published in 2014,
Reprinted in 2017 and 2020
by
Christian Focus Publications Ltd.,
Geanies House, Fearn, Ross-shire,
IV20 1TW, Scotland, U.K.

www.christianfocus.com

Cover design by Daniel van Straaten

Printed by
Bell and Bain, Glasgow

CONTENTS

Foreword 11

1. Young Preacher (c. 1514–47) 15

2. Emerging Force (1547–54) 25

3. Displaced Exile (1554–55) 35

4. Genevan Pastor (1556–59) 47

5. Energized Reformer (1559–60) 61

6. Fearless Defender (1561–63) 75

7. Faithful Preacher (1564–71) 87

8. Tireless Servant (1571–72) 99

9. Enduring Legacy (c.1514–72) 109

Concluding Thoughts 125

*To a fellow laborer and friend who has faithfully
ministered God's Word in this generation,
a treasure to the church in Scotland
and around the world.*

Sinclair B. Ferguson

In the Shadow of Knox

The story of the Protestant movement in Scotland and its extending influence around the world has long been a source of inspiration for me. The most colorful and impactful figure of this pivotal era was unmistakably that of the Scottish Reformer John Knox. As I began to study the life of this spiritual stalwart more carefully in preparation for the writing of this book, I made an unexpected discovery. My research uncovered a personal connection I have with Knox and with St. Giles' Cathedral, the church he pastored in Edinburgh, Scotland – a connection that I had not previously known.

On 9 November 1572, John Knox entered the pulpit at St. Giles' for the final time. As Knox publicly stepped down as the senior minister of this famed church, he laid hands upon his successor, the one who would pick up his mantle and continue his Reformation work. This transfer of authority represented the conclusion of a remarkable period in Scotland's history. Within Knox's lifetime, rising Protestant fervor had inaugurated the spiritual transformation of this storied realm. That successor's name was James Lawson.

By a remarkable providence, my name is Steven James Lawson, my father was James Lawson, and one of my sons is James Lawson. Though I have not verified a direct line to Knox's successor, I, nevertheless, have felt as if I were standing in the shadow of Knox as he laid his hands upon my life.

In keeping with this connection, I had the privilege in the summer of 2013, along with my good friend Sinclair Ferguson, to lead a church history tour through Scotland. While preparing for the trip, we approached the leadership of St. Giles' for permission to hold a private worship service in the Cathedral during our stay in Edinburgh. We were understandably denied. After all, this famed High Kirk cannot open its pulpit to every tourist group that passes through its doors.

However, knowing how meaningful it would be to worship in that hallowed place, I suggested a counter response. I proposed that we tell the hierarchy of St. Giles' that the final time their famed pastor, John Knox, had stood in their pulpit, he had laid his hands on his successor, James Lawson. Another James Lawson was now here to assume the pulpit once again. To my delight, the decision was reversed and permission granted. Our tour group was allowed to hold a worship service within these historic stone walls, and I was permitted to preach in the famed pulpit previously occupied by Knox and Lawson.

Few moments in my life have been more humbling and exhilarating than this grand experience. I was ushered by a beadle, an official servant of St. Giles', through the large front doors of its expansive sanctuary. I was directed to the stairs leading up into the large, carved wooden pulpit, where I found myself elevated above the gathered people. For my text, I chose John 17:3, because Knox testified on his deathbed that this seventeenth chapter of the Gospel of John was where 'I first cast my anchor.' This passage was where Knox first laid hold of Christ by faith. In the exposition of this text, I desired to honor this seminal figure in the history of the Scottish Reformation. By God's grace, I believe that I did.

The more I have studied the extraordinary life and ministry of John Knox, the more significantly he has impacted me. It is as though this bold Scot has laid his hands of influence upon me both as a preacher and, more personally, as a follower of Christ. By the tenacious example of his life, Knox still emboldens me to stand firm as I proclaim the truth of Scripture.

As you read this short account of John Knox's life and ministry, my prayer is that God will impart a similar sway upon your spiritual life. My desire is that you too will be inspired by the courageous faith of this rugged Scot. I trust that as you read these pages, you will encounter more than mere historical facts about a pivotal individual. Instead, my hope is that this life story will ignite your faith in Jesus Christ and inspire you to press forward to serve His kingdom of grace.

I want to express my sincerest thanks to William MacKenzie, the publisher of Christian Focus, and to his nephew, Willie, for their support of this project on the occasion of the 500th anniversary of the birth of John Knox. I want to thank Dr. Rebecca Rine for her editing of the final manuscript before publication. I must also recognize my executive assistant, Kay Allen, who typed this book and helped with its footnotes. Moreover, I would like to thank Dustin Benge, who proved to be invaluable in reviewing and preparing this work.

I thank God for my family that supports me in my life and ministry. My wife, Anne, and our four adult children, Andrew, James, Grace Anne, and John, provide me with much-needed encouragement.

Soli Deo Gloria,

Steven J. Lawson,
OnePassion Ministries,
Dallas, Texas

ONE

Young Preacher

(c. 1514–47)

Wielding astonishing influence over Scotland in the sixteenth century, John Knox (c. 1514–72) was one of the most heroic leaders and towering figures in the annals of church history. Regarded as 'the Father of the Scottish Reformation' and 'the Founder of the Scottish Protestant Church,' Knox was a spiritual *tour de force* of unmatched vigor in spreading the kingdom of God. With resolute convictions, this fiery Reformer established his native land as an impenetrable fortress of biblical truth, one that would reverberate throughout the known world. If Martin Luther was the hammer of the Reformation and John Calvin the pen, John Knox was the trumpet.

Given his immense impact upon Scotland's history and the larger evangelical world, it is time to reintroduce Knox to a new generation of Christian believers. Predominantly forgotten in the modern era, his grave lies beneath a parking lot on the south side of St. Giles' Cathedral in Edinburgh. There is a great need in this present hour for Knox to be resurrected in the memory of all those who share his biblical convictions. This book contributes to that effort by profiling the extraordinary life and powerful preaching of this luminous Scottish Reformer.

At the dawn of the sixteenth century, a thick spiritual darkness veiled the land of Scotland. The religious superstitions of Rome held the nation with an ironclad grip. The Bible was virtually a closed book, and the gospel of grace had been eclipsed by a popish religion of works-righteousness. The clergy groped about in spiritual ignorance as blind leaders of the blind. A famine of the hearing of the Word of God had left the nation impoverished and spiritually emaciated. It was into such a spiritual drought that John Knox, like a Scottish Jeremiah, providentially entered this world.

The early days of John Knox's life did not reveal that he would one day be a leader of his nation and of the church. He was a man of humble beginnings. Though he would receive a fine education and was mentored by men strong in the faith, these traits alone did not set Knox apart or enable him to have such significant impact. The story of John Knox's life is the story of the God who delights in raising up insignificant people to bring glory to His name. The young John Knox was a man like any other. As he placed his life in God's hands, however, he became the mighty trumpet whose clarion call would echo across the land.

Today, Knox's legacy is that of a passionate preacher and prominent Reformer. But before he was a Reformer, he was a 'Reformer in the making.' His skills as an expositor of God's Word and as a prophetic challenger of the status quo were developed over a period of years and even decades. God laid a foundation in Knox's boyhood that would later hold firm through the storms of life, faithfully building him up piece by piece into the man he would become.

Beginnings (c. 1514–35)

John Knox was born around the year 1514 in Haddington, East Lothian, Scotland, which is located about fifteen miles east of Edinburgh.[1] This relatively obscure place was a small town of some 1,500 inhabitants. Knox's parents, members of the Roman Catholic Church, placed a high value upon a proper education and enrolled their son in the local Haddington Grammar School. It was here that his immense intellect first began to be sharpened and shaped.

Knox then entered the prestigious University of St. Andrews (1529), the oldest and one of the most famous universities in Scotland. At the university, Knox studied under the noted theologian, philosopher, and scholar John Major, and he proved to be an ardent student. He graduated from St. Andrews in 1536, earning the M.A. degree, and then taught briefly as an assistant professor. Though there is little record of Knox's activity during these years of study, his later habits of Bible reading and commentary study suggest that he was an avid student and one who thought carefully about theological, political, and social matters. His studies at St. Andrews further honed his intellectual acumen.

Finding His Place (1536–43)

Soon thereafter, Knox was ordained to the priesthood in the Roman Catholic Church by the Bishop of Dunblane (April 1536). Knox so excelled that he took clerical orders even before he reached the age fixed by church canons. As he pressed forward in his new role, he became further entrenched in the same encumbrances of Catholic dogma that had for centuries robbed the Scottish people of the saving knowledge of God.

---

1   The year of John Knox's birth is properly analyzed by Jasper Ridley in Jasper Ridley, *John Knox* (New York and Oxford, Oxford University Press, 1968), p. 531.

Unable to find a parish in which to serve, Knox became a papal notary, a legal officer who could authenticate documents. During this period, the Roman church owned more than half of the real estate in Scotland and gathered an annual income equal to almost eighteen times that of the Scottish crown. Consequently, the position of a papal notary was an important role within the Scottish church.

Knox also served as a private tutor to the sons of two gentry (untitled aristocratic) families in East Lothian from 1540 to 1543. Both families, the Douglases of Longniddry and the Cockburns of Ormiston, were known for their Protestant beliefs. They surely would have exerted some initial gospel influence upon this young, bright teacher. His work with them indicates some openness to these revolutionary doctrines. His experience as a tutor may also have shaped his ability to relate pastorally to others. Though his public persona from the pulpit was often demonstrative, nevertheless he had a pastoral side to his ministry, able to address individuals in light of their own needs and concerns. Thus, while Knox was maturing in his teaching abilities, God had placed him in an environment where he would encounter in a preliminary way the Protestant perspectives that he would one day champion.

Conversion and Growth (1543–44)

The exact time of John Knox's conversion is not known, however it is clear that by the end of March 1543 he was committed to the Christian gospel. His conversion was probably through the preaching of Thomas Guillanne, an ex-Dominican friar and chaplain to the Earl of Arran. Guillanne, it was said, was 'the first man from whom Mr. Knox received any taste of the truth.'[2] At the end of his life, while on his deathbed, Knox would ask his wife to read to him the seventeenth chapter

---

2   David Calderwood, *History of the Kirk of Scotland*, Vol 1, p. 156.

of John. It was there, he said, 'I first cast my anchor.'[3] The truths in this chapter, which records the High Priestly Prayer of our Lord, proved to be the solid rock on which Knox first anchored himself to Jesus Christ by faith alone.

Guillanne also gave Knox his first in-depth exposure to Reformed doctrine. Now recognizing the polluted system of Rome for what it was—contaminated and corrupt—Knox confessed, 'It pleased God to call me from the puddle of Papistry.'[4] For the next two years, Knox devoted himself to the meticulous study of Scripture in a diligent search for a deeper knowledge of the truth.

From Bodyguard to Reformer (1545–46)

As Knox grew in his new faith, George Wishart, a powerful Reformed preacher, began a preaching itinerancy in southern Scotland. When he came to East Lothian, Knox became one of his closest disciples and followers. In a relatively short period of time, Wishart exercised strong influence over Knox in the Reformed faith (December 1545–March 1546). This intense exposure would profoundly shape Knox's ministry for the remainder of his life. From Wishart, Knox learned boldness and courage in ministry, as well as faithfulness to Reformed doctrine in preaching.

As Wishart's ministry gained increasing visibility, his strong preaching drew serious threats upon his life. With supreme loyalty, Knox soon became Wishart's personal assistant and bodyguard. He protected his spiritual mentor with a two-handed sword, ready to defend him to the death.

---

3   William Mackergo Taylor, *John Knox* (New York: A. C. Armstrong & Son, 1885), p. 199.

4   *The Works of John Knox*, ed. David Laing, Vol. 3 (Edinburgh: Bannatyne Society, 1846), p. 439.

By this bold step, Knox's exceptional courage in standing and fighting for the truth first began to emerge.

Religious tension and persecution reached fever pitch in December 1545, and Wishart was arrested and taken to St. Andrews Castle. When Knox attempted to physically defend his mentor, Wishart insisted that he go back to Longniddry. Wishart implored his loyal bodyguard: 'Return to your bairns (pupils), and God bless you. One is sufficient for one sacrifice.'[5]

Wishart was burned at the stake on 1 March 1546, at St. Andrews Castle, by the nephew of the same archbishop, David Beaton, who had in 1528 martyred Patrick Hamilton, the first Reformed preacher in Scotland in this era. As the flames flashed across his body, Wishart cried out:

> I beseech Thee, Father of heaven, to forgive them that have of any ignorance or else of any evil mind, forged any lies upon me. I forgive them with all my heart. I beseech Christ to forgive them that have condemned me to death this day ignorantly.[6]

With these dying words, the gospel beacon was passed to John Knox. The flames that consumed Wishart's body ignited Reformation fires that, by means of Knox, would spread through all of Scotland and Great Britain. Historian William G. Blaikie writes: 'The chief result of this murder was to substitute John Knox for George Wishart, as the man of light and leading for the country…Wishart was to Knox as Stephen had been to Paul.'[7] Though few were aware at the time, the invisible hand of Providence was raising up a new defender of the faith.

---

5   John Knox, *The History of the Reformation of Religion within the Realm of Scotland* (1898, repr.; Edinburgh: Banner of Truth, 2010), p. 58.

6   Ibid., p. 65.

7   William G. Blaikie, *The Preachers of Scotland* (1888, repr.; Edinburgh: Banner of Truth, 2001), pp. 52-3.

Called to Preach (1547)

On 29 May 1546, Cardinal Beaton, the man who had put Wishart to death, was himself assassinated in the same St. Andrews Castle. Previously a Catholic stronghold, St. Andrews increasingly became a rallying point for many who were embracing Reformed teaching. Among those who rallied to the castle, strategically located on Scotland's east coast, were John Knox and his young pupils. In addition to his tutoring responsibilities, Knox also taught Scripture to three students, leading them in a systematic study through the Gospel of John. Others soon joined this class, and the superior nature of Knox's teaching gifts became immediately apparent to all.

Due to his obvious and extraordinary ability in handling the Word, Knox was asked to preach to the congregation that had gathered for worship in St. Andrews Castle. In a sermon preached by John Rough, Knox was publicly charged before the congregation to answer what the former believed to be a divine call upon Knox's life. A startled Knox 'burst forth in most abundant tears, and withdrew himself to his chamber.'[8] Knox strongly believed that he must not run where God had not called him. Locked in his room for days, he underwent much soul-searching until, at last, he stepped forward to answer the call to preach. Knox, now assured of God's summons, presented himself for installation as pastor of the Protestant congregation in the Castle.

Gripped by a sense of direct accountability to God, Knox preached his first public sermon on Daniel 7:24-25 in Holy Trinity Parish Church, St. Andrews. Throughout his exposition, Knox declared his Protestant convictions with unmistakable precision and power. The sermon was delivered with the force

8   Knox, *The History of the Reformation of Religion within the Realm of Scotland*, p. 72.

of a lightning bolt from heaven. It was said by those who heard him, 'Others sned (lop off) the branches of the papistry, but he striketh at the root also to destroy the whole.'[9] Some concluded, 'Master George Wishart never spoke so plainly; and yet he was burnt. Even so will John Knox be.'[10] From this time forward, Knox ministered as a marked man.

After this inaugural sermon, Knox would later affirm that St. Andrews was 'that place where God first in public opened my mouth to His glory.'[11] For the remainder of his life and ministry, Knox asserted, 'I must be blowing my Master's trumpet.'[12] Few preachers in the history of the church have ever sounded forth the Word of God with such intense fervor and stong convictions as did this stout Scot.

Once he had confirmed his inward call and responded to the outward call of the St. Andrews congregation, Knox was unwavering in his certainty that God had summoned and commissioned him to preach His Word. He was deeply convinced of the biblical doctrines of the saving gospel of God and was willing to defend it against all social, political, and religious assaults. As Knox emerged onto the scene, he did so as a valiant force ready to sound

---

9   Knox, *The History of the Reformation of Religion within the Realm of Scotland*, p. 75.

10 Ibid.

11 John J. Murray, *John Knox* (Darlington, England: EP Books, 2011), p. 104.

12 John Knox as quoted by Richard G. Kyle, *The Ministry of John Knox: Pastor, Preacher, and Prophet* (Lewiston, NY: Edwin Mellen Press, 2002), p. 79.

forth the trumpet of God's truth in every corner of darkness.

Later generations of fiery preachers would join their voices to Knox's and herald the full counsel of God whether it was popular or not, without stuttering or stammering. One such preacher was Charles Haddon Spurgeon. This 'prince of preachers' was unashamed to identify with both the great Scottish Reformer and his gospel, saying 'John Knox's gospel is my gospel; that which thundered through Scotland must thunder through England again.'[13]

The early years of Knox's life, considered without knowledge of who he would become, may seem unremarkable or common to some. And indeed, in one sense, they are. The details of Knox's family life and schooling are obscure, and what little we do know does not reveal the depth of what was occurring in his mind and heart during these formative years. What we can say definitively is that God was preparing this man for His service, moment by moment and trial by trial.

---

13   *C. H. Spurgeon Autobiography, Volume I: The Early Years 1834-1859*, a revised edition originally compiled by Susannah Spurgeon and Joseph Harrald (Edinburgh: Banner of Truth, 1973), p. 162.

TWO

Emerging Force

(1547–54)

Like a gathering storm off the shores of Scotland, the spiritual intensity within John Knox was building in strength during the initial years of his ministry. From the moment of his call to preach, the fiery convictions of this unflinching Scot were surging ahead with great force. In an hour when Rome was 'breathing out threatenings and slaughter against all who tried to break them,'[1] Knox was fearlessly preaching the Word of God with the undaunted resolve of the martyrs who preceded him. Nothing could prevent the inevitable Reformation from crashing upon Scotland's coastline, led by this man who would become the most pivotal figure in the nation's history.

---

1   Blaikie, *The Preachers of Scotland*, p. 6.

From the outset of his ministry, Knox firmly believed that to preach the Bible was 'to blow the Master's trumpet.'[2] He viewed himself not as a gentle flute, but as a militant blast, awakening a slumbering nation from its spiritual sleep. As the walls of Jericho came crashing to the ground with the blast of Israelite trumpets, Knox was strongly convinced that it would be the authoritative proclamation of Scripture that would bring down the false religious battlements of this world. It was to such a transcendent view of biblical authority that Knox committed himself throughout the entirety of his ministry.

During the foundational years of his ministry (1547-54), Knox became a marked man. Life-threatening opposition put him at extreme risk. However, through these many dangers God was preparing him to one day establish the Church of Scotland and advance the cause of the Reformation in his native land.

Preaching in St. Andrews (1547)

From his initial preaching in St. Andrews, Knox daringly upheld the cardinal Reformation truth of *sole fide*, that justification is by faith alone in Christ alone. A staunch defender of salvation by grace alone, Knox denounced Rome's teaching on purchased indulgences, holy pilgrimages, forced fasts, and clerical celibacy. He declared these vain practices to be blasphemous and openly pronounced the Pope to be an antichrist. Describing the spiritual climate of the day, William Blaikie explains, 'In those days, every man's preaching was coloured by the attitude he held to the Church

---

2   John L. Murray, *John Knox*, p. 104. John Knox as quoted by Richard G. Kyle, *The Ministry of John Knox: Pastor, Preacher, and Prophet*, p. 79.

of Rome.'[3] As a result, the congregation in St. Andrews renounced Roman Catholicism and pledged their allegiance to the message being preached in the Reformation.

As a lightning rod draws fire, Knox unavoidably attracted the heat of the Roman church for such preaching. He was called before John Winram, the sub-prior of the Augustinians, to give an account of his Protestant doctrine. Knox declared that no man can usurp Christ as the Head of the church, not even the Pope. Moreover, he asserted that Catholic ceremonies went beyond the commands and instruction of Scripture. He insisted that Mass was idolatrous and decried the church's teaching on purgatory. Knox also recognized an insurmountable chasm between the true and false church. But surprisingly, Winram took no action, and Knox was delivered out of the lion's mouth.

Imprisoned as a Galley Slave (1547-49)
In June 1547, St. Andrews Castle came under siege by a fleet of eighteen French galleons. After a month-long attack, the Protestants were bombed into submission and forced to surrender. As their spiritual leader, Knox was a prime target. He was captured, along with 120 other defenders, and consigned to be a galley slave in the hull of a French battleship. For nineteen months (1547-49), he was chained to an oar, with little food, deplorable sanitation, and rampant galley fever. Knox was scorched and blistered in the blazing sun and would shiver on the damp, cold nights. During this long period of intense suffering, Knox grew physically weak, and his health suffered significantly due to the deplorable conditions.

Aboard this ship, repeated efforts were made by his French captors to drive Knox back to Catholicism. On one

---

3   Blaikie, *The Preachers of Scotland*, p. 6.

occasion, a statue of Mary was thrust in his face, and they tried to force him to kiss the image. He resolutely resisted: 'Trouble me not; such an idol is accursed and therefore I will not touch it.'[4] Throwing the icon overboard, Knox vehemently proclaimed, 'Let our Lady now save herself; she is light enough; let her learn to swim.'[5]

On two occasions, Knox rowed in the open water within sight of the steeple of St. Andrews Castle. Longing to stand within her walls once again, he never surrendered his ardent hope that he would one day return and preach where he had first been called to the ministry. With unshakable confidence in the Lord, Knox stated:

> I see the steeple of that place where God first opened my mouth in public to His glory, and I am fully persuaded, how weak soever I now appear, I shall not depart this life till my tongue shall glorify His Holy name in the same place.[6]

Because of the negotiation of the new Protestant King of England, Edward VI, Knox was eventually released from his slavery through a prisoner exchange with France in early 1549. However, it was unsafe for Knox to return to his pro-Catholic homeland, where certain arrest, trial, and, possibly, death would await him. Instead, he journeyed to London, believing Protestant loyalists would welcome him. As expected, Knox was well received, and for the next five years (1549-53), he preached as a Scottish exile in England. His singular mission was now to establish reform in the Church of England.

---

4   Knox, *The History of the Reformation of Religion within the Realm of Scotland*, p. 95.

5   Ibid.

6   Ibid., pp. 95-6.

Pastoring in Berwick-upon-Tweed (1549-51)

At the command of Thomas Cranmer, Archbishop of Canterbury, and the Privy Council, an inner circle of eminent men who advised the king in matters of government, Knox was assigned a pastorate in Berwick-upon-Tweed. This crossroads town was located just three miles from the Scottish border and consisted of some 5,000 inhabitants, half of them soldiers. In April 1549, Knox began pastoring the Berwick Parish Church, also known as the Church of the Holy Trinity. This rugged outpost town proved to be a difficult place in which to minister. In this spiritually dark town, known for moral corruption and licentious living, Knox established the Word of God as a beacon of gospel light.

Through the commanding preaching of Knox, many people in the border town of Berwick were dramatically converted to Christ. Knox would reflect upon the life-changing effect of his preaching:

> God so blessed my weak labours that in Berwick—where commonly before there used to be slaughter by reason of quarrels among the soldiers—there was as great quietness, all the time that I remained there.[7]

In preparation for his sermons, Knox would pore over numerous books and commentaries in personal study of the Scripture. He was convinced that biblical preaching demanded the best mental powers. Thus, he labored to absorb the expository works written by the leading theological writers of ancient and modern times.

On Trial in Newcastle (1550)

The deeper Knox dug into Scripture, the stronger his preaching grew, especially against the idolatrous practice of the Mass.

---

7   Ibid., pp. 276-7.

Accusations by those sympathetic to Catholic dogma were again raised in opposition to him. In April of 1550, he was summoned to Newcastle to give an account for his Reformed doctrine before the Council of the North. Before his examiners, Knox presented a robust biblical defense, stating that 'all worshipping, honouring, or service invented by the brain of man in the religion of God, without his [God's] own express commandment, is idolatry.'[8] Knox's argument was so compelling that no formal charges were made against him. He again was released and returned to Berwick to continue his pastorate.

The town of Berwick is where Knox met his future wife, Marjory Bowes, who was a teenager at the time. Marjory was the daughter of Richard Bowes, the captain of nearby Norham Castle and one of the most influential men in all of northern England. Marjory and her mother, Elizabeth, were converted to Christ under Knox's convicting biblical preaching. Knox and Marjory fell in love and pledged betrothal to one other, though they would not be married until 1555. Marjory would eventually bear him two sons, Nathanael and Eleazar. Later, in Geneva, John Calvin would refer to Marjory as 'a wife the like of whom is not found everywhere.'[9]

Pastoring in Newcastle (1551)
In the early summer of 1551, Knox accepted the call to pastor the Church of St. Nicholas in Newcastle, about 60 miles south of Berwick. Though his time here would be brief, his reputation as a preacher continued to spread, so much so that many fellow Scots traveled across the border to hear him. In the pulpit, Knox's primary focus was on feeding the living Word to his hungry flock. He stated:

---

8   Henry Cowan, *John Knox: The Hero of the Scottish Reformation* (1905, repr.; New York: AMS Press, 1970), p. 105.

9   Lord Charles John Guthrie, *John Knox and John Knox's House* (Edinburgh and London: Oliphant, Anderson, and Ferrier, 1898), p. 56.

I did distribute the bread of life, as of Christ Jesus I received it… My honour was that Christ Jesus should reign, my glory that the light of his truth should shine in you.[10]

Chaplain to the King (1551-53)

With mounting acclaim, Knox was recommended by the Duke of Northumberland to be one of six Royal Chaplains to King Edward VI (1551). This appointment was a significant honor and greatly elevated Knox's influence for the gospel, launching him into itinerant preaching throughout England. Under this Protestant king, Knox took up the task of spreading Reformed doctrine throughout the Church of England.

In September 1552, Knox was asked to move to London, where he frequently preached before the King at such notable places as Windsor Castle, Hampton Court, St. James's Palace, and Westminster Abbey. This strategic placement, Martyn Lloyd-Jones notes, positioned Knox 'right in the centre of affairs in England.'[11] Knox used his increased influence to challenge the prescribed public worship within the Church of England, which, he believed, retained elements of Catholic influence. Knox was convinced that the national church had not gone far enough in its separation from Rome under the previous king, Henry VIII. The political separation was apparent, but the theological separation less so. In Knox's eyes, still more reform was needed.

One area for potential reform concerned the practice of kneeling at communion. The Archbishop of Canterbury, Cranmer, insisted that, when taking communion, one should kneel before the bread and wine. Knox vehemently objected

---

10   Peter Lorimer, *John Knox and the Church of England: His Work in Her Pulpit and His Influence Upon Her Liturgy, Articles, and Parties* (London: Henry S. King & Co., 1875), p. 72.

11   D. Martyn Lloyd-Jones, 'John Knox – The Founder of Puritanism,' *The Puritans: Their Origins and Successors* (1987, repr.; Edinburgh: Banner of Truth, 2002), p. 261.

and denounced this practice as idolatrous, fearing that it resembled Catholicism and failed to conform to Christ. Such protest forced Cranmer to insert in the *Second Book of Common Prayer* (1552) an addition known as the 'Black Rubric,' which clarified that lowering oneself was not an act of worship toward the elements. Because of Knox's insistence, Lloyd-Jones describes him as the 'founder of Puritanism,'[12] or the first to attempt to purify the practices of the Church of England.

With his renown constantly increasing, Knox was soon nominated for the highly regarded bishopric of Rochester (October 1552). Nevertheless, he declined this esteemed position of overseeing many churches, convinced that the Church of England had not reformed enough for him to join it. Instead, he chose to remain 'simply a preacher.'[13] Subsequently, the office of vicar of All-Hallows in Bread Street, London, was also offered to him (February 1553). Again, Knox refused.

Withdrawal into Hiding (1553-54)

On 6 July 1553, the Protestant cause in England came to an abrupt halt. At age sixteen, the reform-minded king, Edward VI, suddenly died. After a nine-day reign by Lady Jane Grey (July 10-19), the Protestants' worst nightmare came to pass. On 19 July 1553, Edward's sister, the strict Catholic, Mary Tudor, was proclaimed Mary I, Queen of England. This succession to the royal throne would ignite persecution fires under a reign of terror for the true believers throughout the nation.

'Bloody Mary,' as she came to be known in future years, slaughtered some 288 of the Reformers, including women and children, and stained England with their blood. Among those burned at the stake would be some of the finest Englishmen of

---

12   Lloyd-Jones, 'John Knox – The Founder of Puritanism,' *The Puritans: Their Origins and Successors* , p. 267.

13   Blaikie, *The Preachers of Scotland*, p. 56.

the day, spiritual leaders such as John Rogers, Hugh Latimer, Nicholas Ridley, and Thomas Cranmer. With such martyrdom looming on the near horizon, Knox withdrew to southern England, where he continued preaching for several months. Finally, in March 1554, he made the agonizing decision to cross the English Channel to the safety of the continent of Europe. There Knox would minister for the next five years.

Little did Knox know that through these tumultuous conflicts, he was becoming battle-tested for the larger campaigns that lay ahead. With every trial and circumstance he faced during these early years, Knox proved himself to be faithful to each divine assignment entrusted to him. In due time, God would entrust this servant of the Word with even greater responsibilities. In his future ministry, Knox's life work would be the establishment of the Church of Scotland. But for now, Knox was found to be a trustworthy steward of the gospel work God had given to him.

THREE

Displaced Exile

(1554–55)

A s fire tempers steel in the glowing flames of a furnace, the heated afflictions in which John Knox constantly found himself were sovereignly used by God to shape and strengthen this chosen servant. From the time of his call into the ministry, Knox lived in the cauldron of smoldering adversity. Nevertheless, it was through these fierce trials that God forged the metal of Knox's character and formed his ironclad convictions. Such difficulty is never an elective course in the school of discipleship, but always a required curriculum. Knox would prove to be no exception. He would pass through countless tests and emerge without even the smell of smoke upon him.

In July 1553, Knox faced one of the most heated conflicts in all of church history as Mary I, the only surviving child born of Henry VIII and his first wife, Catherine of Aragon, ascended to the throne of England. Assuming the Crown, 'Bloody' Mary, as she would be known, abruptly ended the Protestant reforms of her brother, Edward VI. In their place, she asserted her strict Catholic beliefs and vehemently imposed them upon the English people. From 1555 to 1558, Mary's brutal reign of terror resulted in the burning of nearly three hundred Protestant believers at the stake. Commanded to cease their Reformed worship or suffer fatal consequences, these Protestants were be condemned as heretics and torched to death. It was into such a scorching furnace that Knox was placed.

The terrifying regime of Mary I drove Knox to flee England for his life. Already an exile from Scotland in England, Knox now became an exile from England in Europe. This forced departure launched Knox into yet another season of heated trials. Upon this hard anvil, God would hammer him into a sharp instrument that would eventually spread the Reformed movement throughout Scotland. Beginning in 1554, Knox would spend the next six years abroad in Europe, all in preparation for the life work that lay ahead of him, one day, in his native land.

Flight to Dieppe, France (1554)

On 2 August 1553, Mary arrived in London to assume her crown. Her reign of wrath was ready to be ignited for all Protestants who refused her Catholic beliefs. On 16 August, the first two reform-minded leaders were arrested. The prebendary of St. Paul's Cathedral, John Bradford (1510-55), was imprisoned in the Tower of London, and the London preacher and Bible translator John Rogers (c. 1500-55) was confined to house arrest. The next month, the Bishop of

Gloucester and Worcester, John Hooper (c. 1495/1500-55), and the famed Bible translator, Miles Coverdale (c. 1488-1569), were both imprisoned. Hugh Latimer (c. 1487-1555), previously a royal chaplain to King Edward VI, and the Archbishop of Canterbury Thomas Cranmer (1489-1556) were sentenced to the Tower.

These acts of aggression sent many Protestants into hiding and drove others into neighboring countries. With danger lurking, Knox was forced to move about England before fleeing to France (January 1554). For Knox, the decisive issue was whether to refuse the Mass, which he believed was idolatrous, and be martyred, or to escape from England to safety. Though many chose to stay and face the danger, Knox chose exile.

Knox's withdrawal preserved his life, but it also temporarily separated him from his future wife, Marjory Bowes. Conscious that others were giving their lives for the gospel, and fearing that he was a soldier retreating from the battlefield, Knox's departure troubled him greatly. Though it was necessary for the greater cause of the gospel, he nevertheless felt guilty about his withdrawal. Knox wrote:

> I have in the beginning of this battle appeared to play the faint-hearted and feeble soldier (the cause I remit to God), yet my prayer is, that I may be restored to the battle again.[1]

On 20 January 1554, Knox sailed from England to the Continent, landing at Dieppe, France, a thriving port city on the Normandy coast. Ironically, five years earlier, Knox had escaped the French to find refuge in England, and now he was fleeing the English for the safety of France. Knox

---

1   Iain H. Murray, *A Scottish Christian Heritage* (Edinburgh: Banner of Truth, 2006), p. 12.

was there only a few weeks, but managed to write a potent work addressed to the Church of England titled *Admonition to England*.[2] This work was the first of several letters written and published during his European exile. In this treatise, Knox the Reformer pleaded with England not to succumb to the false gospel of Rome:

> O England, England! ... wilt thou yet obey the voice of thy God, and submit thyself to his holy words? Truly, if thou wilt, thou shalt find mercy in his sight, and the state of thy commonwealth shall be preserved.[3]

Using strong language in *Admonition to England*, Knox compared the current Holy Roman Emperor, Charles V, to 'Nero' and declared Mary I of England 'more cruel than Jezebel.'[4] He called for believers 'to flee from idolatry' by refusing to attend Mass. Even if the Government commanded its citizens to take the Mass, Knox exhorted, they must obey the higher authority of God. While in Dieppe, he also finished writing *Exposition of the Sixth Psalm*, a call for the patience of English believers during this time of unjust suffering.

Knox gave serious thought to the political state and spiritual condition of Scotland and England. As he pondered this persecution, he began developing a theological position that entitled citizens under a Catholic monarch to overthrow the Crown with an armed revolution rather than violate the Word of God by taking the Mass. This deep-seated

---

2   The full title is *A Faithful Admonition made by John Knox unto the Professors of God's Truth in England*.

3   John Knox, *Works of John Knox, Vol. 3* (Edinburgh: James Thin, 1854), p. 308.

4   Knox, *The History of the Reformation of Religion within the Realm of Scotland*, p. 99.

conviction would become 'Knox's special contribution to theological and political thought.'[5] Other Reformers, such as John Calvin and William Tyndale, took the opposite side, stating Christians should be subject to their king regardless of circumstances. For Knox, however, a return to popery and the Mass must be resisted at all costs.

Journey to Switzerland (1554)

Leaving Dieppe, Knox traveled across France to Switzerland in order to visit cities sympathetic to the Reformed cause. His goal was to consult the pastors of Protestant congregations concerning whether or not obedience was to be given to a ruler who forces idolatry and condemns true religion. Knox first traveled to Geneva, where he discussed this matter with the leading reformer John Calvin (1509-64). The great French theologian urged submission and caution. Knox next journeyed to Lausanne to meet another noted Reformer, Pierre Viret (1511-71). At last, he made his way to Zurich, where he interacted with the highly regarded reformer Heinrich Bullinger (1504-75). Each of these leaders gave wise counsel and spiritual direction that shaped Knox's thinking and future actions.

This tour complete, Knox returned to Dieppe (May 1554), where he stayed for the next three months, anxious to hear news from England and Scotland. If the news were good, then he might have been able to return and resume his active ministry. But reports from the other side of the Channel were far from encouraging. The situation in England was deteriorating, and the threat of widespread persecution was getting worse. Out of deep concern for those who were being oppressed, Knox wrote two letters during his stay

---

5   Ridley, *John Knox*, p. 171.

in Dieppe: 'A Letter to His Afflicted Brethren in England' and 'A Comfortable Epistle Sent to the Afflicted Church of Christ.' These warm pastoral letters poured forth comfort for all who were persecuted. Knox began the former epistle as follows:

> Dearly beloved in our Saviour Jesus Christ, hope you against hope, and against all worldly appearance. For so assuredly as God is immutable, so assuredly shall he stir up one Jehu or other, to execute his vengeance upon these blood-thirsty tyrants, and obstinate idolaters.[6]

Desiring to expand his grasp of Scripture, Knox traveled back to Geneva in order to sit under the teaching of Calvin and to study Greek and Hebrew. By the late spring of 1554, some 800 English Protestants, rather than face charges of heresy in their homeland, had fled England and taken refuge on the continent of Europe. A large number found safety in major cities in Germany and Switzerland. Among those who found their way to Geneva, 'Europe's city of God,'[7] was Knox.

Tempestuous Pastorate in Frankfurt–on–Main (1554–55)
Knox would not be in Geneva for long. Some 200 Protestants had fled to Frankfurt-on-Main in Germany, a thriving center of commerce and communication, and had established an English-speaking congregation by June of 1554. These refugees included such notables as the future author of *Foxe's Book of Martyrs*, John Foxe (1517-87), the chief translator of the *Geneva Bible*, William Whittingham (c. 1524-79), and

---

6   John Knox, *Select Practical Writings of John Knox* (Edinburgh: Banner of Truth, 2011), p. 111.

7   S. M. Houghton, 'John Knox,' *Puritan Papers, Vol. 4 1965-1967*, edited by J. I. Packer (Phillipsburg, NJ: P & R, 2004), p. 62.

a close pastor friend of Knox's, Christopher Goodman (1520-1603). With a high regard for Knox and his preaching, this gathering of English exiles issued a call for him to be their pastor. Knox sought the counsel of Calvin, who advised him to accept the call. In November of 1554, Knox traveled to Frankfurt-on-Main to become the new church's pastor.

Initially under Knox's pastoral leadership, there was peace among the English exiles in Frankfurt-on-Main. But a controversy soon erupted over the English *Book of Common Prayer*. The issue revolved around using parts of the Anglican liturgy that Knox considered to be idolatrous. Specifically, he believed that kneeling before the sacraments at communion was a blatant sin, a matter he had raised earlier in England with Archbishop Cranmer. Desiring a thoroughly reformed worship service, Knox drew up an 'Order of Service' to replace the *Book of Common Prayer*. In this less liturgical service, Knox refused anything that resembled Rome, including ministerial vestments, the responses of the people to the minister, and other parts of the ornate litany. A small minority of the English members did not support the new worship service, but under Knox's leadership, it was adopted.

As more Marian exiles continued to relocate in Frankfurt-on-Main, an increasing number desired to retain their Anglican liturgy. These new church members pointed to many Protestant leaders who were suffering persecution in England but still supported the old order. To institute a change, they claimed, would disgrace these leaders. Consequently, they argued that worship on the Continent should resemble the face of an English church. To this, Knox countered: 'The Lord grant it to have the face of *Christ's* church.'[8]

---

8   D. Martyn Lloyd-Jones, *The Puritans: Their Origins and Successors* (1987, repr.; Edinburgh: Banner of Truth, 2002), p. 246.

Adding to this conflict, Thomas Lever (1521-77), Master of St. John's College, Cambridge, was installed as the second English pastor in the church. After becoming pastor, Lever would insist upon the old forms of Anglican worship. On 13 March 1555, the situation became intensely worse when Richard Cox (c. 1500-81), previous Chancellor at Oxford, arrived from England and strongly insisted that the liturgy of the Church of England in the *Book of Common Prayer* be followed. The situation turned from bad to worse.

In the face of this crisis, the city leaders initially prohibited Knox from preaching. To preserve peace, they then expelled him from Frankfurt-on-Main. On 26 March 1555, Knox left the city a defeated man. Meanwhile, back in England, Mary I had begun burning the first Reformers at the stake. The first Marian martyr was the Bible translator who had completed Tyndale's work and was lecturer at St. Paul's Cathedral, John Rogers. This valiant figure was burned on 4 February 1555, in Smithfield, London. Five days later, on 9 February, the Bishop of Gloucester and Worcester under Edward VI, John Hooper, and the Rector of Hadleigh, Suffolk, Rowland Taylor (1510-1555), were martyred, Hooper in Gloucester and Taylor in Suffolk.

Return to England, Scotland (1555)

Uncertain about his future, Knox traveled back to Geneva, where he remained for several months. Arriving in April 1555, Knox explained to Calvin what had transpired in Frankfurt-on-Main. Upon hearing this news, the Genevan reformer wrote to Cox and the majority there, rebuking them for their rigid conformity to the *Book of Common Prayer*. Calvin defended his fellow reformer, saying, 'I cannot keep secret that Master Knox was, in my judgment, neither godly nor brotherly dealt with.'[9] This trial served as further preparation for the heated persecution Knox would face, one day, in Scotland.

As Knox arrived in Geneva, an English-speaking congregation was forming, one that he would later pastor. But, presently, Knox had his sights set on another mission. He felt compelled to return to England, where his young bride-to-be, Marjory Bowes, awaited him. From Geneva, Knox traveled across France to Dieppe on the Normandy coast, boarded a ship, and sailed to northern England or, more probably, to Scotland. Arriving in Edinburgh, he was reunited with his fiancée after a three-year absence. The two were joined in marriage in the autumn of 1555.[10]

In Edinburgh, Knox established contact with Protestants in an effort to rally their resolve. At the time, Mary of Guise, the pro-Catholic Queen Regent, governed the Scottish realm. Protestantism was still regarded as heresy, a crime punishable by burning at the stake, though its private practice was somewhat tolerated. Knox was encouraged that small groups of reform-minded believers—known as 'privy kirks,' or private churches—were meeting behind closed doors for Scripture reading and prayer. He exclaimed, 'The fervency here doth far exceed all others that I have seen.'[11] For the next few months, Knox circulated among these groups, giving instruction in the Scripture to these small gatherings and administering the Lord's Supper.

---

9   Lewis Lupton, *A History of the Geneva Bible, Vol. 1: The Quarrel* (London: The Fauconberg Press, 1966), p. 106.

10 Some say the couple was already secretly married before Knox moved to Newcastle in 1551. Others say the marriage took place before he left England in 1553. Most determine it was at this time, either in 1555 or 1556 that they were officially married.

11 Knox, *Works of John Knox, Vol. 4*, p. 216.

The suppression of truth was heightened through a strict ban that had been issued against owning or reading Tyndale's English translation of the New Testament. Nevertheless, Knox discovered that confidence in God's Word and knowledge of biblical truth was spreading underground among the Protestants. He noted:

> Notwithstanding this their tyranny, the knowledge of God did wonderously increase within this Realm, partly by reading, partly by brotherly conference, which in those dangerous days was used to the comfort of many.[12]

Amid this grassroots movement, Knox observed that many Protestants continued to attend Catholic worship and participate in the Mass. He believed such compromise was blatantly idolatrous and inexcusable. In a private debate in Edinburgh, Knox argued convincingly with reform-minded believers that taking the Mass must be forbidden. This bold conviction gained momentum and launched him into a preaching tour to the north of Edinburgh, where he stayed at Dun Castle, an isolated fortress halfway between Montrose and Brechin, during the months of October and November 1555. Wherever he went, Knox discovered a growing interest in Protestantism marked by an intense appetite for biblical truth. Encouraged, Knox traveled south into the Lothians and preached there too.

Concerning Knox's incessant drive to preach, S. M. Houghton writes that this constant movement marked Knox, setting him apart as an energetic figure who was ever moving about, ever advancing the gospel:

---

12   Knox, *The History of the Reformation of Religion within the Realm of Scotland*, p. 58.

> John Knox was primarily a man of action ... In the days of his strength, he loved to itinerate ceaselessly ... [H]e was always preaching in season and out of season.[13]

Such preaching kept Knox in perpetual hot water. His challenge of the present religious order caused the Queen Regent to summon him to Edinburgh in order to answer heresy charges. Few believed this exiled itinerant would actually appear. But when Knox announced that he would indeed attend, many Protestants responded with a pledge to march to Edinburgh and stand with their leader. Once the authorities learned of this plan, the summons was withdrawn. In spite of this, Knox marched on and entered Edinburgh, preaching in many houses the cornerstone truth of the Reformation—justification by faith alone. He asserted, 'The trumpet blew the old sound.'[14]

An Appeal from Geneva (1556)

In Edinburgh, urgent letters were unexpectedly delivered to Knox. This correspondence came from the English-speaking congregation in Geneva, imploring him to return to the city in order to serve as their pastor. As his presence in Scotland was becoming increasingly dangerous, Knox decided to return to Europe, but this time with his wife and mother-in-law. He sent Marjory and Mrs. Bowes ahead by ship to Dieppe, France, to wait for his arrival. After further preaching in Scotland, Knox sailed for the Continent to rendezvous with his new bride and her mother. In July 1556, Knox arrived in Dieppe, determined to return to Geneva to assume his new pastoral duties.

---

13   Houghton, 'John Knox,' *Puritan Papers, Vol. 4 1965-1967*, pp. 60-1.

14   Ridley, *John Knox*, p. 228.

To be sure, the making of a reformer is never easy. Throughout this tumultuous season of Knox's life, his character and convictions were being forged upon the hard anvil of adversity and hammered into steely resolve. The threat of 'Bloody Mary' in England, his conflict in Frankfurt-on-Maine in Germany, and what was a prospective heresy trial in Scotland were providentially used by God to fashion him into the determined leader he would become. Each new difficulty was part of the heated yet necessary preparation that shaped Knox into an intensely focused individual who would lead his countrymen into the knowledge of God's truth. God was deliberately molding this resilient figure who 'bestrode a certain kingdom like a colossus.'[15]

15   Houghton, 'John Knox,' *Puritan Papers, Vol. 4 1965-1967*, p. 59.

FOUR

Genevan Pastor

(1556–59)

idden below street level in the grounds of the University of Geneva, founded by John Calvin in 1559, stands a monument that pays lasting tribute to the Protestant Reformation. Known as the '*Monument international de la Réformation*' or the 'Reformation Wall,' this imposing memorial of statues and bas-reliefs rises 30 feet high and stretches 325 feet in length. Built in 1909 to commemorate the 400th anniversary of Calvin's birth and the 350th anniversary of the establishment of the University of Geneva, it stands for all time as a stark reminder of the history-altering movement that galvanized this ancient city over five hundred years ago.

Emerging prominently from the chiseled granite, standing 15 feet tall, are the four leading figures of the Genevan

Reformation. On the left is the fiery evangelist William Farel (1489–1565), who first lit the match igniting Reformation flames in Geneva. Standing by Farel is the pastor-scholar John Calvin (1509–64), who stoked the flames of Reformed truth through his biblical exposition and extensive writing. To the right of Calvin is his successor, Theodore Beza (1519–1605), the first principal of the Geneva Academy. On the far right is John Knox, dressed in Genevan robe, standing resolutely, Bible in hand, steel-eyed and sober-countenanced.

Knox is the only figure mounted twice upon this famous memorial. He is featured in the middle of the wall and also on a side stone mural, depicted as preaching before an awed congregation at St. Giles' Cathedral, Edinburgh. The sculptor portrays Knox as if he could come flying out of the pulpit in zealous passion for God's truth. This exiled Scot was the man who would carry the Reformation torch back to his native land and emblazon it with the gospel.

While in Geneva, John Calvin played a key role in shaping the future ministry of John Knox. Iain Murray writes, 'It was during Knox's exile, and especially in the final years in Geneva, that the master-principles which governed his thought on Reformation came to maturity.'[1] In other words, the coming Reformation in Scotland had its roots in the time Knox spent in Geneva.

The relatively short period of time that Knox spent in Geneva was a pivotal season that left a lifelong impact on him. Geneva is an international city of refuge made famous by Calvin and the Reformation. It was also the place where Calvin sowed the seeds of biblical truth into his willing co-laborer, seeds that would produce a bountiful harvest upon Knox's return to Scotland.

---

1   Iain Murray, *A Scottish Christian Heritage*, p. 14.

Pastoring in Geneva (1556)

Returning to the Continent from Scotland, Knox arrived in Geneva and was formally admitted to the membership of the English-speaking congregation on 13 September 1556. Although it had been understood that Knox was to be one of the ministers of this congregation on his return, he did not in fact take up his office again until 16 December 1556, when he was re-elected along with Christopher Goodman, who had served in this post while Knox was absent in Scotland during the previous year.

By 1556, the long period of trouble that Calvin had endured at the hands of his enemies the Libertines had passed. In the face of implacable opposition, Calvin had held his nerve, and his strong leadership prevailed. Geneva now enjoyed a period of stability under a reformed government. Based on his own experience of life in the city during these years, Knox found Geneva under Calvin's leadership to be 'the most perfect school of Christ that ever was in the earth since the days of the Apostles.'[2] The life-changing effect of Calvin's preaching of the gospel upon the people was such, Knox exclaimed, as 'I have not yet seen in any other place beside.'[3]

A close friendship quickly developed between Calvin and Knox, leaving a strong impression upon Knox that he would carry with him for the rest of his life. Calvin stirred within Knox an ever greater passion for the glory of God. Biographer John J. Murray notes that it was Calvin's towering, transcendent view of God that emboldened Knox into a spiritual force: 'At the heart of his [Knox's] Christian experience was a vision of God on His throne. Like Calvin,

---

2   Ridley, *John Knox*, p. 215.

3   Ibid.

his great mentor, he lived *coram Deo*, before the face of God.'[4] This theocentric world view, first sparked within Knox in Scotland by George Wishart (c. 1513-46), was fanned into full blaze in Geneva by Calvin. In due course, Knox would return with it to his homeland.

On 16 December 1556, the English-speaking congregation in Geneva installed Knox as their pastor. This flock of displaced exiles had more than one hundred members. Included were many reform-minded Englishmen from Knox's previous church in Frankfurt-on-Main who left after the earlier conflict. In this Genevan church were such notables as William Whittingham, William Williams, Charles Goodman, and John Bodley, whose young son, Thomas, would found the famous Bodleian Library at Oxford. Likewise, many Scottish exiles filled the Genevan church.

Unlike Knox's previous church in Frankfurt-on-Main that insisted on Anglican worship, this Genevan congregation willingly followed Knox's leadership in adopting a reformed order of worship. The regulative principle was implemented. Any practice resembling Rome was forsaken. The Lord's Supper was observed without kneeling. The primacy of the sermon was established. Singing was limited to the inspired words of the Psalms.

According to Scottish historian Thomas Carlyle (1795-1881), this decisive break from the popish practices of the Church of England established Knox as 'the chief priest and founder of ... Puritanism.'[5] Biographer Jasper Ridley makes the same assessment, identifying Knox as 'one of

---

4   John J. Murray, *John Knox*, pp. 103-4.

5   Thomas Carlyle, *Sartor Resartus, and on Heroes, Hero Worship, and the Heroic in History* (New York: P.F. Collier, 1901), pp. 367-8.

the founders of English Puritanism.'[6] Martyn Lloyd-Jones went even further, arguing that Knox was *the* founder of the English Puritan movement:

> In Geneva, therefore, we have the first truly Puritan Church amongst English people… John Knox is the founder of English Puritanism. It was also while at Geneva that he formulated his view with regard to Princes, and the attitude of the Christian towards 'the powers that be.' Here he was ahead of Calvin, and this is again a sign of his true Puritanism. I maintain that one cannot truly understand the revolution that took place here in England in the next century except in the light of this teaching. Here was the first opening of the door that led to that later development.[7]

This season in Knox's life proved to be the most peaceful time he would enjoy. He took great pleasure in married life with Marjory, who bore him a son, Nathanael. Marjory's mother, Mrs. Elizabeth Bowes, lived with them as well in their happy home. Knox was able to study Scripture, read theology, preach the Word, and pastor his flock. Unlike his earlier experience in Germany, his spiritual leadership in Geneva was well received. Gone were the constant conflicts he suffered in Frankfurt-on-Main. Knox relished this period of his life. Nevertheless, despite his present joy, his desire to return to Scotland never waned.

In May 1557, not long after Nathanael's birth, two messengers from Scotland arrived unexpectedly in Geneva to see John Knox: James Syme, Knox's host during his last trip to Edinburgh, and James Barron, a leading merchant in that city. In their possession was a letter signed by four

---

6 Ridley, *John Knox*, p. 236.

7 Lloyd-Jones, *The Puritans: Their Origins and Successors*, p. 275.

Scottish nobles—Archibald Campbell the Lord of Lorne, John Erskine of Dun, Lord James Stewart, and Alexander Cunningham the Earl of Glencairn—requesting his return to Scotland in order to establish a Reformed church based solely upon the authority of Scripture. The letter addressed to Knox read:

> We heartily desire you, in the name of the Lord, that ye will return again to these parts, where ye shall find all faithful that ye left behind you, not only glad to hear your doctrine, but will be ready to jeopard lives and goods in the forward setting of the glory of God, as He will permit.[8]

Knox consulted his congregation and also talked the matter over with Calvin. Should he accept the invitation to return or should he stay and continue his ministry in Geneva? Both were in agreement that Knox must return to Scotland. As he later wrote, he 'could not refuse that vocation, unless he would declare himself rebellious unto his God and unmerciful to his country.'[9] After all, was this not an open door for the extension of the gospel in Scotland? As a result, only eight months after arriving in Geneva, Knox prepared to return to his native land once again.

A Trip to Dieppe (1557)

In September 1557, Knox departed from Geneva for Scotland by way of Dieppe. A month later, on October 24, Knox arrived at this French port city, ready to sail for his native land. However, waiting for him at Dieppe was a second letter from Scotland. This correspondence

---

8   Knox, *The History of the Reformation of Religion within the Realm of Scotland*, p. 129.

9   Ibid., pp. 129-30.

informed him that the Protestant leaders were having second thoughts about the wisdom of his coming to Scotland at this particular time. The letter urged Knox to stay at Dieppe for further instructions.

Knox was shown yet another letter, this one written by a Scottish Protestant gentleman to a friend in Dieppe. The friend was asked to let Knox know about the indecision of the Protestant nobles in Scotland and their reluctance to take any action. In fact, they were reconsidering their previous invitation to Knox due to changes in the political climate. At the time, the Queen Regent was negotiating the marriage of Mary Queen of Scots to the Dauphin of France, and matters had reached a critical stage.

To ensure a satisfactory outcome for the Queen Regent, it was widely expected that generous bribes would be offered to any Scottish lord who supported the project. For Knox, this was just another indication of the greed and self-serving attitude of the nobles. Deeply disappointed and not a little angry, Knox responded with a letter of his own. He appealed to the Scottish Protestant leaders to move forward with the mission for reformation. He waited for a response, but none was forthcoming.

During this stay in Dieppe, Knox received other reports that Bloody Mary continued to burn the English Reformers at the stake. Likewise, the persecution of Protestants in France continued. Enraged by this injustice, Knox wielded his pen and wrote his most impassioned book, *The First Blast of the Trumpet against the Monstrous Regiment of Women*. His intent was to denounce Mary I, who was suppressing the cause of the gospel within her realm. By 'regiment,' Knox meant 'government,' and by 'monstrous,' he indicated 'unnatural.' This forty-five-page diatribe was aimed at what Knox believed to be the unnatural reign of women as monarchs. In the opening words of the Preface, Knox minced no words:

> Wonder it is, that amongst so many pregnant wits as the isle of Great Britain hath produced, so many godly and zealous preachers as England did some time nourish, and amongst so many learned, and men of grave judgment, as at this day by Jezebel are exiled, none are found so stout of courage, so faithful to God, nor loving to their native country, that they dare admonish the inhabitants of that isle, how abominable before God is the empire or rule of a wicked woman.[10]

The opening sentence of the main body began as follows:

> To promote a woman to bear rule, superiority, dominion, or empire above any realm, nation or city is repugnant to nature, contumely to God, a thing most contrarious to his revealed will and approved ordinance, and finally it is the subversion of good order, or all equity and justice.[11]

Most of the book is a stern polemic against the cruelties of Mary I. Knox believed that the recent trials suffered by England and Scotland had come about due to their unbelief and pride. Their tolerance of the Catholic Mass, he declared, had brought the judgment of God upon their lands. The false gospel and the idolatry of popery had provoked God's anger. He claimed that those who resisted attempts to overthrow Mary were resisting God Himself. Little of the book actually addresses the evil of rule by women in general.

---

10 John Knox, 'The Preface,' *Works of John Knox*, *Vol. 4* (Edinburgh: James Thin, 1895), p. 365. [Jasper Ridley, *John Knox*, pp. 268-9.]

11 John Knox, 'The First Blast of the Trumpet against the Monstrous Regiment of Women,' *Works of John Knox*, *Vol. 4* (Edinburgh: James Thin, 1895), p. 372.

So provocative was *The First Blast of the Trumpet* that many of Knox's supporters took issue with it.

Return to Geneva (1558-59)

With no reply from Scotland, Knox departed Dieppe in March 1558 and retraced his steps back to Geneva. Upon his arrival, his previous congregation promptly re-elected him as one of their ministers. In Geneva, Knox poured his substantial energies into preaching the Word and caring for his flock. He and Marjory also had a second son, Eleazar.[12]

Soon after his return in 1558, Knox published *The First Blast* anonymously. The same year, Knox published a treatise that supported the right of citizens to revolt against their ungodly and unjust rulers. Other tracts addressed to Scotland and calling for the implementation of Protestant worship were also written around this time.

Another work of far-reaching consequence with which Knox is associated was a new English version of the Bible known as the *Geneva Bible*. Whether or not Knox had any direct role in the translation itself or in the composition of the marginal notes is unknown. Though published in 1560 under the direction of William Whittingham (c. 1524-79), much of the work was done during 1558 when Knox was back in the city. 'What is certain,' as Ridley points out, 'is that the marginal notes were very largely inspired by Knox's writings and political doctrines. The Geneva Bible was the work of the leaders of the English congregation at Geneva, and they put forward in the notes the political ideas of the two pastors of the congregation, Knox and Goodman.'[13] Ridley maintains that:

---

12   Eleazar was baptized on 29 November 29 1558. His godfather was Miles Coverdale, the venerable Bible translator.

13   Ridley, *John Knox*, p. 288.

> [The] Geneva Bible became the most important instrument of propaganda of the radical Protestants in England and Scotland. Between 1560 and 1644, over 140 editions were published, and it was read in every Presbyterian and Puritan home in both realms. More than Foxe's *Book of Martyrs* or Knox's *History of the Reformation in Scotland*, it influenced the opinions of the English Puritans and Scottish Covenanters.'[14]

This translation would be the Bible of choice for the Reformers and Puritans during the next century and the Bible that the Pilgrims would take to the New World in 1620. Here is another evidence of Knox's significant influence.

Late in 1558, Knox also began writing an extensive work titled *A Treatise on Predestination* that would be published in 1560. This would be Knox's longest, most elaborate work, extending to 468 pages, with some 170,000 words. Knox refuted the Anabaptist criticisms against divine predestination, stating that to reject God's sovereign election was to deny God's omnipotence. Such a position, he believed, was blasphemous. This work is one of the great Reformation polemics against Anabaptist beliefs.

On 17 November 17 1558, the political landscape of England dramatically changed. The staunchly Catholic Mary I died, and her half-sister, a moderate Protestant, Elizabeth I, ascended to the throne. This newly crowned queen proved to be far more sympathetic to the Protestant cause, and the persecution of Protestants immediately stopped. The new queen issued a royal proclamation decreeing all Protestants be released from prison. The English exiles in Europe, including Geneva, were filled with new hope.

---

14   Ridley, *John Knox*, pp. 287-8.

Meanwhile, Knox received more letters from Scotland requesting that he return to his homeland. A group of Scottish Protestants desired Reformed preachers to teach them the Scripture in their homes. They specifically requested Knox to come to lead this Protestant movement. These Scottish leaders also sent a letter to Calvin, urging him to persuade Knox to respond positively to their appeal.

Moreover, with Elizabeth I now upon the throne, the congregation of English exiles in Geneva requested permission from the city officials to return to their homeland. On 24 January 1559, approval was granted, and the exodus began. Four days later, on 28 January 1559, Knox himself left Geneva in order to return to Scotland and champion the cause of the Reformation in his homeland.

Back to Dieppe (1559)

Knox traveled first to Dieppe, arriving on February 19, with the intention of departing on the first available ship for Scotland. Upon his arrival, he discovered that a spiritual awakening was taking place in the coastal city and that the gospel was spreading among the local citizens and officials. He chose to delay his departure for Scotland in order to encourage this work of the Spirit of God. For about six or seven weeks, Knox preached at secret services and presided over private prayer meetings in the town. With every sermon, Knox demonstrated unflinching courage in the face of threatened arrest, imprisonment, and even martyrdom at the hands of the French Catholic authorities. As the revival intensified, the Protestant services could no longer be conducted in secret and were now held in the open. Many were converted and admitted into the church, including numerous prominent citizens.

While in France, Knox wrote to Elizabeth I requesting permission to travel through England *en route* to Scotland. She refused because of his harsh polemic in *The First Blast of the Trumpet*. Further attempts to secure safe passage through England were also unsuccessful, including two appeals by Knox written to Sir William Cecil, Secretary of State under Elizabeth and a sympathizing supporter of the Protestant cause.

Enough time had been spent waiting for a positive reply. On 22 April 1559, Knox boarded a ship bound for Scotland. He arrived in Leith, the port of Edinburgh, on 22 May 1559. This return would mark the beginning of an unprecedented era in the history of his homeland. As Ridley says, 'His greatest hour had come.'[15]. A new day of Protestantism was about to dawn. None could foresee what God's providence had prepared for Knox. The reverberation of reformed doctrine in Scotland would eventually be felt from the royal palace to the most humble cottage.

John Knox is rightly associated with John Calvin and Geneva in the unfolding influence of the Reformation upon Western civilization. During the brief time Knox spent with Calvin, the great Genevan Reformer's teaching took root within his fertile mind. Though Knox's stay in the Swiss city was relatively short, he nevertheless experienced something of the reality of the city's official motto,

---

15   Ridley, *John Knox*, p. 314.

post tenebras lux, or 'after darkness, light.' Under Calvin's expository ministry, the light of the flaming torch of truth broke through the thick fog of popery that had long shrouded the city in darkness. At last, the true gospel of grace was shining brightly upon the people. Their hearts were illuminated by its transforming truth. Knox had witnessed this first hand, and he would never forget what he saw.

With this blazing torch in hand, Knox set his face toward Scotland. Rightly has biographer Thomas M'Crie called Knox 'the light of Scotland.'[16] The dark night of biblical ignorance had prevailed far too long. This tenacious torchbearer would journey back to his beloved homeland and ignite a new Reformation with the saving message of sovereign grace.

---

16   Thomas M'Crie, *Life of John Knox* (Philadelphia: Presbyterian Board of Publication, 2004), p. 342.

FIVE

Energized Reformer

(1559–60)

After twelve tumultuous years in England and Europe, John Knox returned to his homeland in 1559, never to leave again. The events of the intervening years from his capture in St. Andrews in 1547 had uniquely qualified him for what would prove to be a defining hour in Scottish history. God had prepared the man for the moment and the moment for the man. Knox was now singularly focused upon 'the reformation of religion and suppressing of idolatry.'[1] The time for the thorough reformation of the church in Scotland had come. According to Martyn Lloyd-Jones, Knox was

---

1   John Knox, Letter to Anne Locke, 29 June 1559, *The Works of John Knox, Vol. 6* (Edinburgh: James Thin, 1895), p. 30.

> a man for his age; a man for his times. Special men are needed for special times; and God always produces such men. A mild man would have been useless in the Scotland of the sixteenth century, and in many other parts of this country. A strong man was needed, a stern man, a courageous man; and such a man was John Knox .... In those times an heroic rugged character was needed; and God produced the man.[2]

Upon returning to Scotland, Knox discovered that the land of his youth was in a deplorably low spiritual state. Fresh courage and strong leadership were essential if the stranglehold of false religion was to be broken. Knox did not flinch at the challenge. S. M. Houghton, echoing the words of the prophet Jeremiah's commissioning, describes Knox as a man 'called of God to root out, to pull down and to destroy, to throw down, to build and to plant, a work which he did right nobly.'[3] Knox's goal was indeed to uproot Roman Catholicism from Scottish soil and to plant biblical Christianity in its place.

Given this imposing challenge, it is hardly surprising that Knox is a hotly debated figure and has long been regarded as 'one of the most controversial figures in history.'[4] Knox was a rugged and resolute individual, tenacious in his efforts to reshape the course of a nation. Despite his rough edges, he became the father of the Scottish Reformation and the founder of modern Scotland. In his nation's darkest hour, he touched the Reformation torch to the powder keg of monarchial religious control and ignited explosive change across the land.

---

2   Lloyd-Jones, 'John Knox—The Founder of Puritanism,' *The Puritans: Their Origins and Successors*, p. 279.

3   Houghton, 'John Knox,' *Puritan Papers, Vol. 4 1965-1967*, p. 59.

4   Iain Murray, *A Scottish Christian Heritage*, p. 5.

Landing at Leith (May 1559)

After a six-year exile in Europe, Knox landed at Leith, the port of Edinburgh, on 2 May 1559. Scotland was still Roman Catholic and was governed by the French Queen Regent, Mary of Guise. Although she had held this position since 1554, she had done little to stand in the way of the reform of the church. But with her daughter Mary Queen of Scots now married to Francis, the Dauphin of France who had also been given the title 'King of Scots', she now took bold action against the growing reform within the country. Backed by the presence of French military, Mary of Guise suppressed any Protestant cause in her realm, determining that no individual could preach or administer the sacraments without permission from the Catholic bishops. She had reform-minded Scottish preachers arrested, tried, and threatened with the death penalty.

On the very same day that Mary of Guise issued a summons against four Scottish preachers on the charges of usurping ecclesiastical authority and preaching heresy and sedition, Knox's ship docked at Leith. The Catholic bishops were already assembled in the city for a provincial synod, but they were not prepared to act against the well-known Protestant 'heretic' without orders from the Queen Regent, who at that time was about fifty miles away in Glasgow. By the time they had communicated with her, Knox had already left the city for Dundee. As he contemplated the conflict that lay ahead, Knox wrote:

> [It is] uncertain as yet what God shall further work in this country, except I see the battle shall be great for Satan rageth even to the uttermost.[5]

---

5   Knox, *The Works of John Knox, Vol. 6*, p. 21.

Preaching at Perth (May 1559)

Knox next traveled west to Perth, a town sympathetic to Reformation truths, with the intention of preaching the gospel. It was through Perth, a town called 'the centre of the Reformation movement,' that William Tyndale's English Bible had been smuggled into Scotland (1527) and where George Wishart had preached before his martyrdom (1544).

Knox's preaching in Perth was an act of open defiance to Mary's royal decree. Knox passionately confronted the sins of apostate faith, religious deceit, and the idolatry of the Mass. Knox described his sermon of 11 May as 'vehement against idolatry,'[6] and it certainly had the effect of rallying Protestant sympathizers to break the yoke of Roman tyranny. Shortly after the sermon had ended, a priest entered the church to celebrate Mass. A riot broke out, and the church altar, images, and ornaments were destroyed. Knox condemned the action of 'the rascal multitude'[7] as extreme, but no one, it seemed, could repress the escalating anger of the people. In the aftermath, the Charterhouse and the houses of the Black and Grey Friars, Catholic monasteries, would suffer irreparable damage, and within weeks, monasteries in St. Andrews, Crail, Cupar, Stirling, Linlithgow, Edinburgh, and Glasgow would likewise be ransacked.

Mary of Guise was enraged by the destruction of the church in Perth. To resist the uprising, she dispatched 2,000 troops, most of whom were French, to suppress the rebels. Scottish noblemen responded quickly by raising an even larger army, and were prepared to withstand the soldiers under Mary's command. To prevent a bloodbath, an outcome that neither

---

6   Knox, *The History of the Reformation of Religion within the Realm of Scotland*, p. 164.

7   Ibid.

side wanted but which seemed inevitable if the fighting continued, a truce was signed. However, the Queen Regent soon broke her agreement and sent her troops into Perth. This heavy-handed aggression only provoked more Scottish noblemen to align themselves with the Protestant cause. These leaders, known as the 'Lords of the Congregation,' resolved to defeat Mary and establish the Reformation in Scotland.

Preaching in St. Andrews (June 1559)

From Perth, Knox traveled throughout Fife, preaching in various towns and openly rebuking the Queen Regent for her unscrupulous actions. In the fishing village of Anstruther, another iconoclastic revolt took place. Knox then travelled the short distance to St. Andrews so that he could fulfill his long-cherished hope of preaching in the town where he had received his call to the Christian ministry. Fearing for his safety, Knox's advisors warned against this bold advance. Armed French troops were camped only a few miles away. Moreover, Archbishop Hamilton had sworn that if Knox tried to preach in St. Andrews, 'he should make him be saluted with a dozen [muskets].'[8] However, this Protestant firebrand could not be denied and responded fearlessly:

> My life is in the custody of Him whose glory I seek. Therefore I cannot so fear their boast nor tyranny, that I will cease from doing my duty, when of His mercy He offereth me the occasion. I desire the hand or weapon of no man to defend me.[9]

---

8   John J. Murray, *John Knox*, p. 59.

9   Knox, *The History of the Reformation of Religion Within the Realm of Scotland*, pp. 175-7.

On 11 June, a Sunday, Knox entered his former pulpit at the parish church of St. Andrews and preached to a large congregation. His sermon was on Jesus' cleansing the temple of the buyers and sellers. The implications were unmistakably clear: the Scottish church must throw off all vestiges of papal religion. So powerful were his sermons on this and three subsequent days that large numbers of local citizens renounced Catholicism, as did as many as twenty-one priests. The tide was turning.

Knox traveled throughout the region, preaching forcibly, and was met with the same encouraging results. 'The trumpet soundeth all over,' Knox wrote as the power of the Word was being unleashed.[10] 'We do nothing but go about Jericho, blowing with trumpets as God giveth strength, hoping victory by his power alone.'[11]

Referring to this period of spiritual awakening, nineteenth-century historian William Blaikie observes, 'The degree of force brought into play by such convictions in a vehement nature like Knox's is beyond calculation.'[12] Even Knox himself was amazed at this rapid advancement of the truth. John Calvin recognized the notable advancement of the gospel in a personal letter to John Knox, writing, 'We are astonished at such incredible progress in so brief a space of time.'[13] By the power of the Spirit and through the preaching of men such as Knox, the cause of the Reformation was rapidly gaining ground.

---

10   Knox, *The Works of John Knox, Vol. 6* (Edinburgh: James Thin, 1895), p. 78.

11   Ibid.

12   Blaikie, *The Preachers of Scotland* , p. 62.

13   John Calvin, *Tracts and Letters, Vol. 7: Letters, Part 4, 1559-1564*, edited by Jules Bonnet, translated by Marcus Robert Gilchrist (1858, repr.; Edinburgh: Banner of Truth, 2009), p. 73.

Minister at St. Giles' Church, Edinburgh (July 1559)

After only two months in Scotland, Knox was appointed the minister of St. Giles' Church[14], Edinburgh, on 7 July 1559. As the High Kirk of Edinburgh, this was the most important pulpit in the land.[15] St. Giles' was to be the focal point of Knox's ministry for the rest of his days, except for a brief period spent in St. Andrews in the late 1560s. For over a decade, Knox would deliver his most powerful sermons in this grand edifice, including many condemnations of Queen Mary for her practice of Mass.

From the pulpit of St. Giles', Knox preached to as many as 3,000 worshipers. His sermons during this period have been described as possessing 'considerable scholarship, immense familiarity with Scripture, good acquaintance with ancient history, and great fervor of spirit.'[16] In what is no doubt a tragic loss to preachers of later generations, only one transcript of these messages survives. Nevertheless, Knox's stalwart voice can almost be heard as he challenges his fellow Scots to declare their highest allegiance to God:

> Wouldest thou, O Scotland have a king to reign over thee in justice, equity, and mercy? Subject thou thyself to the Lord thy God, obey his commandments, and magnify thou the word that calleth unto thee, 'This is the way, walk in it' (Isa. 30), and if thou wilt not, flatter not thyself; the same justice remains this day in God to punish thee, Scotland, and thee Edinburgh especially, which before punished the land of Judah, and the city of Jerusalem. Every realm or

---

14 St Giles was not a cathedral in Knox's day. It was a kirk but became a cathedral when the first bishop was appointed to the church of St Giles by King Charles I in 1635.

15 This imposing cathedral is prominently located on the renowned Royal Mile between Edinburgh Castle and the Palace of Holyroodhouse.

16 William M. Taylor, *The Scottish Pulpit: From the Reformation to the Present Day* (Birmingham, AL: Solid Ground Christian Books, 2004), p. 47.

nation, saith the prophet Jeremiah, that likewise offendeth, shall be likewise punished (Jer. 9).[17]

Preaching in Stirling (November 1559)

Knox's strong influence and bold preaching escalated rather than lessened the political and religions tensions in Scotland. A civil war was looming. The Queen Regent wanted to subdue Scotland to the rule of France and to crush the Protestant Reformation in favor of Roman Catholicism. The Lords of the Congregation responded by taking up arms against Mary in support of religious freedom. However, their military campaign suffered a devastating setback when they failed in their attempt to take the port of Leith. With spirits deflated, many soldiers in the Protestant army returned to their homes, while those who remained withdrew with their leaders to Stirling. This was perhaps the darkest hour of the Reformation in Scotland.

Knox left his pulpit in Edinburgh and accompanied the dispirited troops to Stirling. Seizing the first opportunity presented to him, he preached at the Church of the Holy Rude from Psalm 80:4-8, determined to instill fresh hope and courage in the hearts of his downcast congregation of Protestant forces.

> I doubt not but this cause, in despite of Satan, shall prevail in the realm of Scotland. For, as it is the eternal truth of the eternal God, so shall it once prevail, howsoever for a time it may be impugned.[18]

Many believed Knox's words, and his remarkable sermon became one of the turning points of the Scottish Reformation. The soldiers were revived and filled with renewed hope. They

---

17   Knox, *The Works of John Knox, Vol. 6*, p. 241.

18   Ibid. *Vol. 1*, p. 473.

were once again confident that with God's help, victory would surely come, in spite of whatever setbacks, disappointments, and hardships they must endure. The impact of the sermon at Stirling is evidence that Knox was far more than a mere teacher of truth. He was an earnest preacher whose holy zeal stirred the souls and arrested the hearts of his hearers. In a letter to Knox, written in November 1559, John Calvin acknowledged this arousing effect of Knox's preaching:

> I am not ignorant how strenuous you are in stirring up others, and what abilities and energies God has endowed you with for going through with this task [of preaching].[19]

The Scots Confession (August 1560)

On 11 July 1560, the cause of the Reformation took a sudden turn for the better when the Queen Regent, Mary of Guise, died in Edinburgh Castle. By this timely providence, Scotland was saved from a protracted conflict. The Treaty of Edinburgh was signed on 6 July which prepared the way for the withdrawal of French troops from Scottish soil and for all religious questions to be settled by the Scottish Parliament. Within a few weeks, Parliament passed the legislation that abolished the Catholic religion in Scotland and established Protestantism as the religion of the state. Papal authority was abolished, and Mass was made illegal. Anyone attending Mass was to be punished by confiscation of property and imprisonment for a first offence, and faced banishment and death for repeated breaches of the law.

To further reinforce this new stance, Parliament commissioned Knox to form a committee of theologians who would draft a confessional statement that would become the

---

19   John Calvin: *Tracts and Letters, Vol. 7*, p. 73.

theological standard of Scotland. Knox appointed five men to serve with him, each having the name 'John.' Serving under Knox's leadership, these devoted men, known as the 'Six Johns,'[20] wrote the *Scots Confession* in only four days. On 17 August 1560, the document was ratified by Parliament, and on 24 August, the legislation came into force. All previous statutes against Protestant 'heretics' were repealed. Thus, Scotland became a Protestant state.

The Preface to the *Scots Confession* states that the infallible Word of God is the exclusive authority of the church. This assertion of *sola Scriptura*, the formal principle of the Reformation, was a declaration that, since Scripture is the sole source and standard of all doctrine, all religious traditions must yield to biblical truth. This rule applied to the *Scots Confession* itself, which also must come under the scrutiny of Scripture:

> If any man will note in this our Confession any article or sentence repugnant to God's Holy Word, that it would please him of his gentleness, and for Christian charity's sake, to admonish us of the same in writing; and we, upon our honour and fidelity, do promise him satisfaction from the Holy Scriptures, or due reformation of that which he shall prove to be amiss.[21]

The *Scots Confession* remained the church's confession of faith for almost one hundred years, when it was superseded by the Westminster Confession in 1647. Reformed truth had been officially embraced as the theological norm of the nation.

---

20 The others were John Spottiswoode, John Row, John Willock, John Douglas, and John Winram.

21 Thomas Martin Lindsay, *The Reformation* (1882, repr.; Edinburgh: Banner of Truth, 2006), p. 117.

Treatise on Predestination (1560)

The year 1560 also saw the publication of Knox's *Treatise on Predestination*. This lengthy work refuted the doctrines of the 'Anabaptist' or 'Radical' Reformation and had been written during the author's stay in Geneva (1558-59), where it was also published. For Knox, the absolute sovereignty of God was the firm foundation of all he believed and taught. He confidently maintained the supremacy of God over creation, providence, salvation, and judgment. God alone exercises unrivaled authority over the kings and queens of this world. This cornerstone truth gave Knox the unflinching courage to face the overwhelming challenges of his day.

Knox understood the Scriptures to teach clearly God's unconditional election of sinners for salvation. He asserted that the eternal destiny of the elect is made certain by sovereign grace: predestination, justification, and glorification are inseparably bound together. The final salvation of the elect is unalterably secure:

> [God's] love toward his elect [is] always unchangeable; for as in Christ Jesus he has chosen his church before the beginning of all ages, so by him will he maintain and preserve the same unto the end.[22]

In the face of inward doubt and paralyzing fears, Knox was persuaded that the doctrine of predestination is a firm anchor for the soul:

> There is no way more proper to build and establish faith, than when we hear and undoubtedly do believe that our election, which the Spirit of God doth seal in our hearts, consists not in ourselves, but in the eternal and immutable good pleasure of God.[23]

---

22   Knox, *The Works of John Knox, Vol. 6*, p. 267.

23   Ibid., *Vol. 5*, p. 26.

Knox maintained that, in the midst of life's difficulties, the knowledge of divine teaching on predestination brings great assurance to the sincere believer: 'Unless the very cause of our faith be known our joy and comfort cannot be full.'[24] He was clearly persuaded that the doctrine of election, rightly understood, infuses strength into the believing soul. This foundational doctrine would thunder from Scottish pulpits and transform the mindset of a nation.

The First Book of Discipline (1560)

In addition to his other duties, Knox became the primary author of *The First Book of Discipline,* a document which aimed to establish the polity of the Reformed church in Scotland. Along with *The Book of Common Order*, it formed the original *Church Order of the Reformed Church of Scotland.*

In this work, Knox, along with the other contributors, stated that God's Word should be understood according to 'the plain reading or interpretation of the Scripture.'[25] Moreover, he established a congregation's right to elect its own minister. Further, he ordered the proper administering of the sacraments, the ministry of elders, the practice of church discipline, and the appointment and service of deacons. This important document outlined what would become a distinctly Presbyterian form of elder-led polity. After centuries of spiritual darkness, the rays of divine truth were beginning to shine across the land to illuminate hearts.

Amid these encouraging developments, Knox suffered a most painful loss. In December 1560, his young wife Marjory, only twenty-seven years of age, died. She left behind

---

24 Knox, *The Works of John Knox, Vol. 5*, p. 26.

25 Knox, *The History of The Reformation of Religion within the Realm of Scotland*, p. 253.

their two young sons, Nathanael and Eleazar. His mother-in-law, Mrs. Bowes, would continue to live in the household and assist in raising the children. The soul-crushing experience of losing his beloved spouse was felt deeply. Observing Knox's response to this bitter and heavy blow, Calvin wrote a letter of condolence to the grieving Knox, and also told a mutual friend, 'Although I am not a little grieved that our brother Knox has been deprived of the most delightful of wives, yet I rejoice that he has not been so afflicted by her death as to cease his active labours in the cause of Christ and the Church.'[26]

From the moment Knox planted his feet back on Scottish soil, he wielded a monumental influence on the spread of the gospel. His impact was empowered by an uncompromising commitment to the Word of God. As he stood in the pulpit, he saw himself as an instrument in the hand of God, a trumpet that must sound a clear and clarion call to the nation. As Iain Murray has noted: His authority came from the conviction that preaching is God's work, the message is His word, and He was sure the Holy Spirit would honor it.[27]

In this difficult hour, Knox raised his voice and spoke with unwavering confidence in the truth.

---

26   Knox, *The Works of John Knox, Vol. 6*, p. 125.

27   D. Martyn Lloyd-Jones & Iain H. Murray, *John Knox and the Reformation* (Edinburgh: Banner of Truth, 2011), pp. 124-5.

Through his bold proclamations, Knox was used to call a nation back to God. It was his divine assignment to lead his fellow countrymen out of spiritual darkness into the light of God's truth.

SIX

Fearless Defender

(1561–63)

Upon returning to Scotland, John Knox had emerged from the furious rage of Mary I to face another Mary—Mary of Guise. When this latter Mary died in 1560, there was yet another Mary he must confront— Mary Stuart, the newly crowned queen of Scotland. The daughter of King James V of Scotland and Mary of Guise was born in 1542, and her father died just six days after her birth. As the royal heir-in-waiting, she was sent to France for her own protection. At the young age of fifteen, she married Francis II, the Dauphin, and spent her adolescence abroad in France in the glitter of luxurious palaces and castles.

Upon the death of her mother, Mary Stuart officially became Mary, Queen of Scots. When Mary was seventeen, Francis II unexpectedly died. A year later, Mary returned to

Scotland as Queen. On 19 August 1561, she received a warm reception from the Scots who had gathered at Leith to welcome her ashore. Beautiful, intelligent, and forceful, the new Queen was also staunchly Catholic. The battle for the hearts and minds of the Scottish people was far from over.

First Sermon against Mary (31 August 1561)

Mary did not wait long to insist on her right to have Mass celebrated in the chapel royal at the Palace of Holyroodhouse, Edinburgh. On 24 August 1561, the Sunday after her return to Scotland, Mass was given at Holyrood, the door of the chapel being guarded by Lord James Stewart. When Knox heard about this, he was not at all impressed with the defense Lord James offered, that he was preventing 'all Scottish men to enter in to the Mass.'[1]

Mary's action was not only a flagrant breach of the Act passed by the Reformation Parliament of 1560. In Knox's view, this Mass was a dangerous precedent, which, if not forcefully resisted, might lead to the reintroduction of the old religion and a new wave of persecution against Protestants. More importantly, the Mass was a blasphemous act, an offence to God which merited His judgment upon the nation that tolerated it. The following Sunday, Knox thundered a warning from the pulpit of St. Giles':

> One Mass...is more fearful to me than if ten thousand armed enemies were landed in any part of the Realm of purpose to suppress the whole Religion. In our God there is strength to resist and confound multitudes if we unfeignedly depend upon Him, whereof heretofore we have had experience. But when we join hands with idolatry, both God's amicable

---

1   Knox, *History*, p. 268.

presence and comfortable defence leaveth us, and what shall then become of us?[2]

Thus, before nearly all the Scottish nobility and his large congregation, Knox denounced the idolatry of Mary's Mass. Included in the congregation was the English ambassador Thomas Randolph, who wrote a week later in a letter to the Secretary of State, William Cecil:

> I assure you, the voice of one man [Knox] is able in one hour to put more life in us than five hundred trumpets continually blustering in our ears.[3]

Such was the extraordinary effect of Knox's bold stance. His one voice was louder and more compelling than an entire regiment of trumpeters.

For Knox, one Mass meant that French soldiers would surely be sailing for Scotland in order to empower Mary. The next day, the Privy Council decreed that Mary must uphold the Protestant faith or be subject to the death penalty.

First Confrontation with Mary (4 September 1561)

News of Knox's rebukes soon reached the Queen's ears. She immediately summoned the preacher to appear before her in the royal palace. The following Thursday, 4 September, Knox made his way down the Royal Mile to the Palace of Holyroodhouse for what was to be the first of several interviews with Mary.

In the presence of Lord James Stewart, the Queen accused Knox of several things. He had stirred up the people against her mother, the late Queen Regent, and against herself. In addition, he had written a book against her lawful authority,

---

2 Knox, *History*, p. 270.

3 Knox, *The History of the Reformation of Religion within the Realm of Scotland*, quoting Randolph to Cecil 7 October 1561, p. 283.

a reference to Knox's *The First Blast of the Trumpet against the Monstrous Regiment of Women*. Moreover, he was the fomenter of rebellion and bloodshed in England.

Knox patiently listened to Mary and then proceeded to give a lengthy rebuttal of her charges. The Queen also questioned him about his views regarding the obedience due to rulers. Knox responded:

> If their princes exceed their bounds, Madam, no doubt they may be resisted, even by power. For there is neither greater honour, nor greater obedience, to be given unto father or mother. But the father may be stricken with a frenzy, in which he would slay his children. If the children arise, join themselves together, apprehend the father, take the sword from him, bind his hands, and keep him in prison till his frenzy be overpast—think ye, Madam, that the children do any wrong? It is even so, Madam, with princes that would murder the children of God that are subjects unto them.[4]

Mary retorted, 'Well then, I perceive that my subjects shall obey you and not me; and shall do what they list, and not what I command; and so must I be subject to them, and not they to me.'[5] Knox exclaimed, rather, that supreme loyalty belongs to the crown of heaven:

> God forbid that ever I take upon me to command any to obey me, or yet to set subjects at liberty to do what pleaseth them! My travail is that both princes and subjects obey God.[6]

After further discussion about the 'true' church and the monarch's duty toward it, Mary declared that she would defend her Church at all costs. To this, Knox boldly replied:

---

4   Knox, *The History of the Reformation of Religion within the Realm of Scotland*, p. 279.

5   Ibid.

6   Ibid.

Your will, Madam, is no reason; neither doth your thought make that Roman harlot to be the true and immaculate spouse of Jesus Christ. Wonder not, Madam, that I call Rome an harlot; for that Church is altogether polluted with all kind of spiritual fornication, as well in doctrine as in manners.[7]

The Queen challenged him, 'Ye interpret the Scriptures in one manner, and they interpret in another. Whom shall I believe? Who shall be judge?'[8] This was Knox's confident response:

Madam, ye shall believe God, [who] plainly speaketh in His Word...The Word of God is plain in itself. If there appear any obscurity in one place, the Holy Ghost, which is never contrarious to Himself, explaineth the same more clearly in other places.[9]

Frustrated with Knox's reply, Queen Mary expressed her wish that certain learned Catholic teachers were present to challenge his reasoning. Knox remained undeterred:

Madam, would to God that the learnedest Papist in Europe...were present with Your Grace to sustain the argument; and that ye would patiently abide to hear the matter reasoned to the end! Then, I doubt not, Madam, but ye should hear the vanity of the Papistical Religion, and how small ground it hath within the Word of God.[10]

This concluded the first encounter between Queen Mary and Knox. But the matter was far from settled. In November of 1561, Mary defiantly celebrated the Mass with excessive pomp

---

7   Knox, *The History of the Reformation of Religion within the Realm of Scotland*, pp. 279-80.

8   Ibid., p. 280.

9   Ibid.

10   Ibid., p. 281.

and splendor. This display prompted Knox and the Scottish preachers to intensify their polemics against the Queen.

Second Confrontation with Mary (15 December 1562)

About a year later, Knox was disturbed to hear a report that Mary had enthusiastically celebrated news of the renewal of persecution of Huguenots in France. Mary's uncle, the Duke of Guise, had butchered forty Protestants attending a prayer meeting at Vassy in Champagne. The next Sunday, 15 December 1562, Knox preached a scathing sermon regarding the vanity of rulers and 'the pleasure they take in the displeasure of God's people.'[11] Knox condemned Mary's celebratory dancing as a particularly distasteful kind of gloating over the destruction of God's children. Two days later, the Queen summoned the preacher to appear before her. Upon his arrival, she charged him with attempting to make her look bad in public and to turn her subjects against her. She also stated that, if she did something in the future of which he disapproved, then he must come to her in private rather than rebuke her in public. Knox retorted:

> I am called, Madam, to a public function within the Church of God, and am appointed by God to rebuke the sins and vices of all. I am not appointed to come to every man in particular to show him his offence; for that labour were infinite. If your Grace please to frequent the public sermons, then doubt I not but that ye shall fully understand both what I like and mislike, as well in your Majesty as in all others.[12]

By this abrupt response, Knox made it clear it was not his duty to give private admonition to his ruler. Instead, he chose

---

11   Knox, *The History of the Reformation of Religion within the Realm of Scotland*, p. 304.

12   Ibid., p. 305.

to treat Queen Mary like any other person. Knox denounced from the pulpit the sins of all without any discretion, whether those of potentates or of parishioners.

Third Confrontation with Mary (11 April 1563)

Just a few months later, on Easter (11 April 1563), a number of priests in the west of Scotland were arrested by the local Protestant lairds for celebrating Mass. Mary received a report of their action while at Lochleven Castle and summoned Knox to appear before her there. The Queen addressed him at length and prevailed upon him to influence the Protestants not to punish others for their religious observances.

Knox answered that if the Queen would enforce the laws of Scotland, she would have nothing to fear from the Protestants, for they would not take the law into their own hands. But if she did not, he was afraid that there would be some who would fill the void to ensure the law was kept and justice done. 'Will ye allow that they shall take *my* sword in their hand?' Mary asked indignantly. Knox replied:

> The Sword of Justice, Madam, is *God's*, and is given to princes and rulers for one end, which, if they transgress, sparing the wicked and oppressing innocents, their subjects, who in the fear of God execute judgment, where God hath commanded, offend not God, neither do they sin that bridle Kings from striking innocent men in their rage…
> It shall be profitable to Your Majesty to consider what is the thing Your Grace's subjects look to receive of Your Majesty, and what it is that ye ought to do unto them by mutual contract. They are bound to obey you, and that not but in God: ye are bound to keep laws unto them. Ye crave of them service; they crave of you protection and defence against wicked doers. Now, Madam, if ye shall deny your duty unto them, who especially crave that ye punish

malefactors, think ye to receive full obedience from them?
I fear, Madam, ye shall not.[13]

The next day, the Queen and Knox met again. She reluctantly
decided to enforce the Scottish law against Catholic offenders
who openly celebrated the Mass. Knox feared that Mary
would change her mind. To reassure her, he reminded her that
if she indeed upheld the law in this case, she would 'enjoy rest
and tranquillity within your Realm; which to Your Majesty is
more profitable than all the Pope's power can be.'[14]

Fourth Confrontation with Mary (May 1563)

In May of 1563, Queen Mary was advancing plans to marry
Don Carlos, son of Philip II of Spain. Due to Spain's strong
ties with the Pope, Knox feared that this royal union would
bring about a resurgence of Catholic dominance within
Scotland. Knox preached forcibly against this prospective
union from his pulpit at St. Giles'. He declared to his
congregation, populated with Scottish nobility:

> I hear of the Queen's marriage ... But this, my Lords, will
> I say—note the day, and bear witness after—whensoever the
> Nobility of Scotland professing the Lord Jesus, consents that
> an infidel—and all Papists are infidels—shall be head to our
> Sovereign, ye do so far as in ye lieth to banish Christ Jesus from
> this Realm. Ye bring God's vengeance upon the country.[15]

Both Catholics and Protestants alike were angered by this
sermon. Mary ordered Knox to appear at the royal palace for
yet another interview. As the face-to-face encounter began,

---

13   Knox, *The History of the Reformation of Religion within the Realm of Scotland*,
      p. 317.

14   Ibid., p. 320.

15   Ibid., p. 328.

the Queen melted in a flood of tears. She challenged his right to question her marriage: 'What have ye to do with my marriage? Or, what are you within this commonwealth?'[16] Knox famously responded as follows:

[I am] a subject born within the same, Madam. And albeit I neither be Earl, Lord nor Baron within it, yet God hath made me—how abject so ever I be in your eyes—a profitable member within the same, yea, Madam, to me it appertains no less to forewarn of such things as may hurt it, if I foresee them, than it does to any of the nobility; for both my vocation and conscience crave plainness of me.[17]

One noted Knox biographer argues that, with this pointed answer, 'modern democracy was born.'[18] Mary was obviously not pleased with his response. She responded with an emotional outburst and uncontrollable sobbing that continued for some time. Finally, Knox spoke:

Madam, in God's presence I speak. I never delighted in the weeping of any of God's creatures. Yea, I can scarcely well abide the tears of my own boys whom my hand correcteth; much less can I rejoice in your Majesty's weeping. But seeing I have offered to you no just occasion to be offended, but have spoken the truth, as my vocation craves of me, I must sustain, albeit unwillingly, Your Majesty's tears, rather than I dare hurt my conscience, or betray my Commonwealth through my silence.[19]

Queen Mary could no longer bear this interview with Knox. Knox was commanded to leave the cabinet room and wait in

---

16   Knox, *The History of the Reformation of Religion within the Realm of Scotland*, p. 330.

17   Ibid., p. 331.

18   Ridley, *John Knox*, p. 426.

19   Knox, *The History of the Reformation of Religion within the Realm of Scotland*, pp. 331-2.

an adjoining chamber. It soon became clear that the interview was over, and Knox returned to his home.

Fifth Confrontation with Mary (October 1563)

On 8 August 1563, despite laws restricting the practice of Mass, many Catholics in Edinburgh, some of whom had reluctantly but regularly been attending Knox's sermons at St. Giles', gathered for Mass at Holyroodhouse. This observance ignited no small firestorm. The next Sunday, 15 August, Protestants with firearms marched to the royal chapel. A number of Catholics were arrested and sent to trial.

The Queen retaliated by bringing charges against Patrick Cranstoun and Andrew Armstrong, two of the protestors, for forcible entry, violence, and riot in breaking into the chapel. Knox, in turn, wrote to Scottish Protestants throughout the nation, calling on them to come to Edinburgh for the trial on October 2 in support of their persecuted brothers. As it happened, the trial of the two Protestant men was adjourned, and no further proceedings were taken against them, or, it seems, against the Catholics who had attended the Mass at Holyroodhouse. But Mary did take action against Knox.

In December 1563, Knox was arraigned before Privy Council on a charge of high treason for having called the Queen's subjects to assemble without lawful authority. A large number of his St. Giles' congregation accompanied him to Holyroodhouse in order to lend their support. This was the last time that Knox and Mary would meet.

In contrast to the Queen, who by turns wept and laughed uncontrollably, the Reformer was in complete control of himself and his emotions. Though standing before the Queen and her Privy Councillors, he acquitted himself competently and refused to be cowered. 'I am in the place where I am demanded of conscience to speak the truth, and therefore the truth I speak, impugn it whoso list.' Mary, Queen of Scots must have thought him 'an old fool,' but C. J. Guthrie, editor of Knox's *History of the Reformation*, is surely right to see him as he truly was, a man of 'heroic spirit.' In a footnote, he reminds the reader of words Knox had spoken on an earlier occasion—words that so perfectly sum up his sense of conviction on this occasion:

> As for the fear of danger that may come to me, let no man be solicitous. My life is in the custody of Him whose glory I seek. Therefore I cannot so fear their boast or tyranny that I will cease from doing my duty, when of His mercy He offereth me the occasion. I desire the hand or weapon of no man to defend me. Only do I crave audience. Which, if it be denied here unto me at this time, I must seek further where I may have it.

And in a letter to his mother-in-law in 1553, he breathes the same heroic spirit:

> Never can I die in a more honest quarrel than to suffer as a witness of that Truth whereof God has made me a messenger.[20]

> Throughout Knox's tempestuous life, this rugged Scot was never any bolder than when he stood before Mary, Queen of Scots. Whenever summoned to appear in her royal presence, Knox asserted that he spoke to her in God's presence. He

20   Knox, *The History of the Reformation of Religion within the Realm of Scotland,* p. 346.

never once backed down from her, nor did he ever hesitate to speak frankly. By these confrontations, Knox proved to be a man who was not a mere people-pleaser. Mary once commented, 'I am more afraid of his [Knox's] prayers than an army of ten thousand men.'[21] Knox was unwavering in his commitment to the Word of God. Without any hesitation, he said:

> I am not master of myself, but must obey Him who commands me to speak plain, and to flatter no flesh upon the face of the earth.[22]

Even as Knox stood for the truth, the support of his colleagues and friends was beginning to diminish. When he returned to Scotland in 1559, both the nobility and commoners quickly supported him. But in the escalating battle for the soul of the nation, large numbers of Protestants showed signs of weakness. Many wavered in their commitment to the vital truths and cause of the Reformation. Yet despite this vacillation, Knox stood firm, held to his convictions, and strove to advance the Reformation movement in Scotland.

---

21 John Howie, *The Scots Worthies* (1870, repr.; Edinburgh: Banner of Truth, 2001), p. 57.

22 Knox, *The History of the Reformation of Religion within the Realm of Scotland*, p. 330.

SEVEN

Faithful Preacher

(1564–71)

Wherever John Knox found himself, he was inevitably embroiled in a gathering storm. Nowhere was this more true than when he returned to Scotland after his years in Europe. Back in his homeland, he constantly lived in a world full of political intrigue, conspiracies, assassination attempts, secret agreements, royal scandals, private informants, diplomatic negotiations, royal weddings, civil revolts, and open revolution. Such things as these marked the next period in the life of Knox. Following his famous confrontations with Mary, Queen of Scots, a time of upheaval beyond anything seen before in Scotland engulfed the nation. Amid this uproar, Knox had come into the kingdom for such a time as this.

Throughout this turbulent period, Knox remained the bold and faithful preacher he had always been. From his pulpit in Edinburgh, this 'Protestant watchdog'[1] proved to be the single most influential force for the Reformation in Scotland. Iain Murray notes, 'But for the resolution and courage of Knox, the whole Reformation might have failed.'[2] This is to say, Knox was raised up by God to be the primary instrument in the preservation of the Protestant cause in Scotland.

Knox proved to be a lighthouse for Reformed truth, a rudder for the church in Scotland, and an anchor for the cause of true religion in the nation. This notable leader provided direction and stability even in the turbulent seas in which Scotland found itself.

Marriage to Margaret Stewart (25 March 1564)

On Palm Sunday, 25 March 1564, Knox married his second wife, Margaret Stewart, the daughter of his old friend Lord Ochiltree. Knox was aged fifty and Margaret just seventeen. During the sixteenth century, this age discrepancy was not uncommon. But what was surprising was the social mismatch, for Margaret was a member of the royal house of Stewart, Queen Mary's own family. She was a descendant of an earlier king of Scotland, James II. Her uncle had married the sister of King Henry VIII, and widow of James IV, Margaret Tudor. That the son of a Haddington merchant should marry someone of the Queen's own family was bad enough, but that he should be a renegade priest and her dreaded enemy was infuriating to Mary, and she threatened to drive Knox out of Scotland once again.

Upon their marriage, Knox chose to send his two sons to the safety of England, where they would be raised under

---

1   Ridley, *John Knox*, p. 418.

2   Iain Murray, *A Scottish Christian Heritage*, p. 19.

the watchful and loving care of their maternal grandmother, Elizabeth Bowes. Margaret Stewart would bear Knox three daughters and would survive her husband by some forty years.

Before the General Assembly (June 1564)

In June 1564, the General Assembly convened in Edinburgh, where a public debate took place between Knox and the Queen's supporters. In this open dispute, Knox was charged with labeling Queen Mary a slave of Satan and inciting the people of Scotland against her. Knox defended himself, saying that Mary was a rebel against God, an idolater who obstinately persisted in the celebration of Mass.

The chief adversary against Knox, Maitland of Lethington, asserted that Mary was at least sincere. That is to say, she was convinced that her practice of Mass was good religion. Without wavering, Knox countered with the observation that the idolatrous Israelites who had offered their children to Moloch were also convinced that their religion was right. But the truth is that such religion is false. It does not honor God, but is a form of rebellion against Him.[3]

> The disputation soon turned to the duty of subjects to obey or resist a wicked ruler. Knox stated his conviction that the people of a nation invite divine punishment upon themselves if they follow the sins of the ruler. He cited multiple Old Testament examples in support of his position, arguing that loyal subjects are duty-bound to resist the tyranny of an evil prince. For example, he believed it lawful for citizens to refuse obedience to a king's command to kill innocent people. Knox contended that, if the people obey such an order, they themselves become murderers and guilty before God. Moreover, God sometimes orders subjects to rise up

---

3   Ridley, *John Knox*, p. 435.

against their ruler and take vengeance upon him or her. Knox maintained that sitting upon the throne does not give one immunity to the law: 'I find no more privilege granted unto kings by God, more than unto the people, to offend God's Majesty.'[4]

Preaching in Edinburgh (August 1565)

Throughout these tempestuous years, Knox continued his preaching ministry at St. Giles' in Edinburgh, holding not only the common people but also the Queen and her courtiers accountable to God and His Word.

Though Mary had a long history of contending with Knox, she soon had other domestic and political affairs to command her attention. When her cousin, Elizabeth, learned of her marriage negotiations with Don Carlos of Spain, she sent word to Matthew Stewart, the Earl of Lennox, and his son Henry, Lord Darnley. The eighteen-year-old Darnley, a Roman Catholic, was Mary's first cousin and had family ties to the royal houses of both Scotland and England. In time, Mary took interest in Darnley and abandoned her plans to marry Don Carlos.

In spite of the forebodings of some Scottish Protestants and Elizabeth's change of mind, Mary married Darnley in July of 1565. She also conferred on him the title of King, making him the next heir to the throne if Mary died childless. The following month, King Henry entered St. Giles' in great pomp to hear Knox preach, sitting on a throne made especially for him. But the sermon he heard that day was not to his liking. In fact, he was greatly offended by it. Knox cited an unfavorable Old Testament reference to the evil King Ahab and to women rulers. He made it clear that authority is

---

4   Ridley, *John Knox*, p. 436.

not given to rulers to use however they desire. Instead, their royal position must be used in compliance with the purposes and the law of God. Knox declared:

> Kings, then, have not an absolute power to do in their regiment what pleaseth them; but this power is limited by God's Word; so that if they strike where God commandeth not, they are but murderers; and if they spare when God commandeth to strike, they and their throne are criminal and guilty of the wickedness that aboundeth upon the face of the earth for lack of punishment.[5]

The King was so angered by Knox's doctrine that he ordered Knox to appear before the Privy Council that very night. Darnley rebuked the preacher and forbade him to preach whenever the Queen or he was in Edinburgh. However, the Edinburgh council resisted the order as unreasonable for a preacher. They decided that Knox should be allowed to preach whatever and whenever he desired. The order was never enforced. But already the conflict between Knox and the King was apparent.

History of the Reformation (1566)

In 1566, Knox continued writing his monumental work, *The History of the Reformation within the Realm of Scotland*. This remarkable piece, originally dictated to secretaries, provided a history of the dramatic events of the Scottish Reformation. He had first begun this project in 1559 as a narrative of the extraordinary transformational events that were taking place in his native land. This labor would be his major literary contribution and lasting legacy. It would not be completed until shortly before his death in 1571 and would not be published in full until 1644. *History* was the most widely

---

5   Knox, *The Works of John Knox, Vol 6*, p. 238.

read of Knox's writings. Written in vivid language and aggressive tone, this work has the detail and style that only an eyewitness and participant could offer. In it, Knox ascribed the remarkable work of reformation entirely to God:

> God hath honoured us so, that men have judged us the messengers of the Everlasting. By us hath He disclosed idolatry, by us are the wicked of the world rebuked, and by us hath our God comforted the consciences of many.[6]

Travels to England (December 1566)

In December 1566, Knox obtained permission from the English Government to cross the border into England. The purpose of his journey was twofold. First, he wanted to visit his two sons, who were living under the care of Elizabeth Bowes in Durham or Northumberland. Second, Knox desired to help a number of the younger English Puritans who were rigorous in their opposition to vestments and other superstitious practices within the Church of England. These younger Puritans looked to Knox as their mentor and to the Church of Scotland as their model. Knox counseled the troubled leaders to take a moderate course of action, remaining in the Church of England and supporting the message of salvation being preached there. He would later write, 'God forbid that we should damn all for false prophets and heretics that agree not with us in our apparel and other opinions, that teacheth the substance of doctrine and salvation in Christ Jesus.'[7]

During Knox's visit to England, the house in which Darnley was residing at Kirk o' Field, just outside Edinburgh, was blown up. The next morning, his body was found in

---

6   Knox, *Works, Vol. 6*, p. 423.

7   Ibid.

the garden, and it appeared that he had died, not from the explosion, but from strangulation. The scene had all the signs of a conspiracy. The chief suspect was James Hepburn, the Earl of Bothwell, one of Mary's lovers. The Queen and the Earl, who was a Protestant, were married three months later.

The Scottish nobility refused to support this union between Mary and the Earl, and they revolted against their Queen. On 15 June 1567, Mary surrendered to the lords at Carberry Hill, though Bothwell managed to escape by fleeing to Norway. Mary was brought to Edinburgh, where her angry subjects called for her execution. She was then taken to Lochleven and imprisoned there.

Return to Edinburgh (25 June 1567)

Knox returned to Scotland on 25 June 1567, and resumed his preaching in St. Giles'. In his sermons he called for Mary to be tried for her part in the death of her husband and executed if found guilty. Knox insisted that the Queen was subject to the law of God and that that law required the death penalty for those guilty of murder. These messages led to an uprising against Mary, the first modern revolution by the people against the purported 'divine right of kings.'

On 25 July 1567, the Scottish lords went to Lochleven Castle, where Mary remained a captive. Their intent was to pressure her to relinquish the throne to her thirteen-month-old son, James, by signing an official document. Under duress, Mary acquiesced, and the infant James was recognized as the new king of Scotland.

Preaching at King James VI's Coronation (29 July 1567)

On July 29, Knox preached the coronation sermon for James VI in the parish church of Stirling. His text was taken from the Book of Kings on the ascension of the young King Jehoash. Later, in 1603, after Elizabeth I, Queen of England, died childless, James would become King James I of England and Scotland. This infant monarch-in-waiting was the King James who would commission and publish the King James Bible (1611).

The Parliament of December 1567 marked the triumph of Knox and the church. A prolific number of statutes were passed in the two weeks this Parliament sat, and among these were nineteen which had the effect of establishing Protestantism and the church more firmly than before. The legislation of 1560 was now ratified, the Confession of 1560 became the official religious doctrine of the nation, and the Protestant Church of Scotland was, according to Knox, the only true Church of Jesus Christ within the realm.

On 2 May 1568, Mary escaped from Lochleven. She raised an army of 6,000 men, but it was soundly defeated on 12 May at Langside, near Glasgow. Mary fled to England for asylum, and she lived there under the protection of Queen Elizabeth I for the next nineteen years until 1587, when she was executed following her implication in a plot to assassinate the Queen. In her absence, the acting authority for the Scottish government passed to Mary's half-brother, Lord James Stewart, the Earl of Moray. He was appointed Regent until the young king, James VI, came of age.

Continued Ministry in Edinburgh (1568)

Knox, now 54 years of age, remained physically active in his labors for Christ. However, the many strenuous years of escalating conflict accelerated a decline in his health. He nevertheless maintained a rigorous preaching schedule, preaching twice on Sundays at St. Giles and three times during the week. In addition, Knox traveled throughout Ayrshire, Fife, and the south of Scotland, functioning as an unofficial overseer of ministers.

As the recognized leader of the reformed Church of Scotland, he offered pastoral counsel and support at each place he visited. Wherever he went, he preached in the parish church and assisted in resolving various church difficulties. The heavy demands of such a schedule began to take a toll on his body.

On 21 January 1570, Moray, a committed Protestant known as 'the Good Regent,' was tragically assassinated. This was a devastating setback for the Reformed cause. The funeral was held in St. Giles' on Tuesday, 14 February, and attended by 3,000 mourners, including the Scottish nobility who supported King James VI. Knox presided over the service and preached a powerful sermon. He remained supportive of young King James and urged the other ministers to pray for him, for some still supported Mary and a growing number were hesitant to take sides in what was becoming an increasingly bitter conflict over political control of Scotland.

In the autumn of 1570, Knox suffered a stroke that caused him to temporarily lose his capacity of speech. His enemies, who remained loyal to Mary, claimed that he had been struck by divine vengeance. But the rapidly aging preacher made a complete recovery and returned to full faculty in his pulpit ministry.

In this time of political upheaval, large numbers of Scottish citizens still held to the old Catholic religion. Knox saw the political battle between the King's supporters and the Queen's loyalists as a conflict between Protestantism and Catholicism. In other words, the political battle was tied in with a larger spiritual conflict. For Knox, supporting King James VI was a just cause because it entailed support of the true gospel. At the same time, he believed that those who aligned themselves with the Queen were committing a crime of treason that was worthy of death.

Mounting Conflict in Edinburgh (1570)

Tensions between the King's lords and the Queen's lords escalated, and forces loyal to the Queen soon took control of Edinburgh Castle. William Kirkcaldy, Captain of the Castle and one of Knox's longest-standing friends and allies, suddenly shifted his allegiance to Mary. Kirkcaldy then launched military offensives against the city of Edinburgh, where many Protestant supporters of King James lived; the close proximity of the fighting put Knox in grave danger.

On Sunday, 24 December, Knox deplored Kirkcaldy's actions from the pulpit at St. Giles', saying:

> To see stars fall from Heaven, and a man of knowledge to commit so manifest treason, what godly heart cannot but lament, tremble and fear?... Within these few years men would have looked for other fruits of that man than now buddeth forth.[8]

Kirkcaldy issued a protest against Knox's sermon to the Kirk Session of Edinburgh, but Knox continued denouncing him in the pulpit, assailing him as a murderer. Knox also continued to rebuke the Queen. Knox's congregation rightly feared for his life and posted a guard outside his house. A rifle shot was fired through the window of his house, which would have killed him if he had been in his usual chair.

On 30 April 1571, other pro-Mary forces joined Kirkcaldy in Edinburgh Castle. Recognizing that he was in a position of strength, the Captain declared that all supporters of King James must leave Edinburgh immediately. On 4 May, his soldiers demolished part of St. Giles' Church lest it be used as a military fortress by the forces of King James. It was now too dangerous for Knox to remain within the city.

On 5 May 1571, under the influence of the appeals of friends, Knox reluctantly withdrew from Edinburgh with

---

8   Ridley, *John Knox*, p. 495.

his wife, his three young daughters, Martha, Margaret, and Elizabeth, and his secretary, Richard Bannatyne. They crossed the Firth of Forth to Abbotshall in Fife. In July, they traveled to St. Andrews, where Knox would spend the next thirteen months of his life. Knox had become so weak by this point that he was unsure if he would survive the trip.

Through these many dangers, Knox persevered in his ministry, boldly preaching the Word and trusting God for the outcome. Beneath his frail body was an unshakable confidence in the sovereignty of God. He believed that his times were appointed for him by an all-powerful God. He knew that he was invincible within the allotted time of the divine will. His faith remained strong in the One who orders all things.

As Knox approached his final years, his commitment to God grew yet deeper. The opposition he faced never subsided, even to the end, but neither did his confidence in God.

EIGHT

Tireless Servant

(1571–72)

In His inscrutable providence, God's invisible hand sovereignly ushered onto the stage of human history the right servant at the right time to lead the right cause. When the church is at its lowest ebb, when its work is most waning, when error sits on the throne and truth is chained in the dungeon, God brings to the forefront an individual with unusual godliness and giftedness, a person who is able to galvanize the divine cause and lead the charge. John Knox was such a man, a rugged figure fit for the times who fanned the flame of the Scottish Reformation.

Arthur Herman, writing in *How the Scots Invented the Modern World*, makes the following estimate of this indomitable individual:

Just as the German Reformation was largely the work of a single individual, Martin Luther, so the Scottish Reformation was the achievement of one man of heroic will and tireless energy: John Knox. Like Luther, Knox left an indelible mark on his national culture. Uncompromising, dogmatic, and driven, John Knox was ... a preacher of truly terrifying power ... a Protestant firebrand.[1]

To the end of his life, Knox remained firmly entrenched in the cause of the Reformation in Scotland. As this energetic Reformer approached his final years, he did not become a retiring figure, retreating into the shadows to escape resistance. Neither did Knox become mellow in his latter days, losing his sharp edge. Instead, Knox persisted as a resolute figure who persevered in the effort to establish a Reformed church in Scotland. As Knox approached the final days of his life, he remained stout of heart and strong in conviction. Though his outer man was perishing, his inner man was being renewed day by day.[2]

Over the final months of his life, Knox remained a faithful soldier of the Lord, manning his post and fighting the good fight of faith. It has often been said it is not how one starts the race, but how one finishes that counts most. By this estimate, Knox was a triumphant servant in the causes to which the Lord had enlisted him. He remained in the battle to the end of his life.

Returning to St. Andrews (July 1571)

In 1571, though Queen Mary had abdicated her throne and fled into exile in England, her pro-Catholic party in Scotland remained intent on restoring her to the throne. The assassination of the Earl of Moray in 1570 gave new hope to this movement. As a result, the civil war within Scotland escalated national tensions to such a level that Knox was forced to withdraw from Edinburgh to ensure his safety. On

---

1   Arthur Herman, *How the Scots Invented the Modern World* (New York: Crown Publishers, 2001), p. 13.

2   Cf. 2 Corinthians 4:16.

5 May 1571, he left Edinburgh with his wife, three daughters, and personal secretary, Richard Bannatyne, and traveled to St. Andrews. Stopping several times along the way, in July he entered the town where he had first been called to preach. An ill and frail man, he would remain in St. Andrews for the next thirteen months, preaching in the local parish church.

Despite his declining strength during this period, Knox preached virtually every day in St. Andrews. This was especially notable given how weak he had become with age. He became so frail that he could barely walk to church, and wherever he went, he limped, leaning on a staff in his right hand, with his helper, Bannatyne, supporting his left arm. These two steadying forces stabilized him and helped him move along the streets of the town.

Once Knox arrived at the church each day, he had to be assisted into the pulpit. Though fragile in body, Knox's strength was renewed by God in the moment of preaching. He would begin deliberately, but by the end of the sermon he was so energized that he would preach with the fervor of his earlier days. Observers noted that as Knox expounded the Scripture, it seemed he was about to smash the pulpit into pieces and be catapulted out of it! This endurance was all the more remarkable given the vast loss of health and strength that he had recently experienced.

James Melville (1556-1614), a teenage student, heard Knox's preaching at St. Andrews in 1571 and was enthralled by his energetic delivery. He described the great Reformer's preaching as follows:

Of all the benefits that year [1571], was the coming of that most notable prophet and apostle of our nation, Mr. John Knox, to St. Andrews … I heard him teach there the prophecy of Daniel, that summer and the winter following. I had my pen and my little book and took away such things as I could comprehend. In the opening up of his text he was

moderate for the space of half an hour; but when he entered
to application, he made me so to grew (shudder) and tremble,
that I could not hold a pen to write. He was very weak. I saw
him, every day of his doctrine, go slowly and warily, with
a fur…about his neck, a staff in one hand, and good, godly
Richard Ballantyne, his servant, holding up the other, from
the abbey to the parish kirk and, by the same Richard and
another servant, lifted up to the pulpit, where he behoved to
lean at his first entry, but before he had done with his sermon,
he was so active and vigorous, that he was like to ding [hit]
the pulpit in blads [pieces], and fly out of it.[3]

The young Melville was not alone in his admiration for Knox.
Other students also held the aged preacher in highest regard.
Reflecting three decades later, Melville still remembered
Knox as 'that extraordinary man of God.'[4] Knox would enter
the college yard, sit down on a bench, and engage the students
in spiritual conversation. He challenged them to expend
themselves fully for the cause of the gospel. He exhorted them
to invest their time and energies wisely for the cause of Christ.
Knox himself exemplified these very exhortations.

Writing Last Will and Testament (13 May 1572)
Knowing his ill health could not sustain him for long,
Knox wrote his last will and testament at St. Andrews on
13 May 1572. After a parting word to the Papists and to the
unchanging world, he stated:

A dead man have I been almost these two years last bypast, and
yet I would that they should ripely consider in what better estate
they and their matters stand in, than it has done before … But

---

3   Knox, *The Works of John Knox, Vol. 6*, p. xlviii.

4   J. Melville, *The Autobiography and Diary of Mr. James Melville, Minister of
     Kilrenny in Fife and Professor of Theology in the University of St. Andrews* (ed. R.
     Pitcairn) (Edinburgh, 1842) (written in 1600), p. 33. [Jasper Ridley, *John
     Knox* (New York and Oxford: Oxford University Press, 1968), p. 504.]

because they will not admit me for an admonisher, I give them over to the judgment of Him who knows the hearts of all.[5]

Last Ministry to Edinburgh (August 1572)

On 31 July 1572, the parties of King James and Queen Mary entered into a truce, thus ending the civil war in Scotland. The King's supporters could now return to Edinburgh and resume their lives in peace and safety. Among those coming back to Edinburgh was Knox, who returned at the urging of his former congregation at St. Giles'. In August, the aging preacher and his family arrived in the city where he had so courageously preached and served. His physical condition had declined so dramatically that the relatively short journey took longer than expected.

Upon his arrival in Edinburgh, Knox preached in St. Giles' on 31 August for the first time in sixteen months. However, his voice was so weak that he could not be heard in the large sanctuary. From that point forward, the declining preacher spoke where he could be heard in a smaller room attached to St Giles', known as the Outer Tolbooth. Despite the lessening of his voice's projection, the passion within his soul remained intense. During the last weeks of his life and ministry, Knox preached on the crucifixion of Christ from Matthew 27. This was 'a theme,' says Thomas M'Crie, 'with which he had often expressed a wish to close his ministry.' To the very end, Knox was preaching Christ and Him crucified, exalting his Savior and extolling his Lord.

Due to deteriorating health, Knox realized a difficult choice was inevitable. He simply could not continue his pulpit ministry. Therefore, he must make plans to step aside and pass the duty to the next man. On 7 September, he wrote to James Lawson (c. 1538-84), the Sub-Principal at the University of Aberdeen and a gifted preacher, only thirty-two years of age,

---

5   Knox, *The Works of John Knox, Vol. 6*, pp. lv, lvii.

and summoned him to Edinburgh. James Melville called him 'a man of singular learning, zeal, and whom I never heard preach but he melted my heart with tears.'[6] Knox believed Lawson was the one person who should succeed him. Sensing the end of his life was fast approaching, Knox added to his note, 'Make haste, my brother, otherwise you will come too late.'[7]

Final Exhortation in St. Giles' (9 November 1572)

On 9 November 1572, Knox stood in the pulpit of St. Giles' for the final time. After preaching at the Outer Tolbooth, he entered the High Church to preside over the installation of his successor, Lawson. Following the service, Knox hobbled away on his staff, returning to his house at Trunk's Close on the Royal Mile, never to enter St. Giles' again. Moreover, he was never to leave the house again.

Two weeks before his death, Knox was too weak even to sit in a chair. However, mistakenly thinking it was the Sabbath, Knox insisted on getting out of bed. Having preached Christ's crucifixion a few weeks previously, he intended to go to the church in order to preach on what would have been his next subject, the resurrection of Christ. He had been meditating on the resurrection of the Lord throughout the night. To the end of his days in ministry, this aged figure maintained a singular focus upon Christ.

By Thursday, 13 November, Knox was so weak he could no longer read the Scripture, a practice that had been his daily discipline. He asked Bannatyne to read John 17 aloud. It was this chapter that God had used years earlier to bring him to personal faith in Christ. Further, Knox desired to hear Isaiah 53, the great Old Testament chapter prophesying the substitutionary death of Christ for sinners. Finally, he

---

6   James Melville, in William Blaike, *The Preachers of Scotland*, p. 71.

7   Knox, *The Works of John Knox, Vol. 6*, p. 652.

had Bannatyne read a chapter from Ephesians, verses which underscored the sovereign grace of God's saving purposes in his life. He also wanted several sermons of John Calvin read aloud to him in French. The godly influence of the Genevan reformer was with him until the end.

The next day, Knox's strength momentarily recovered, and he rose out of bed. Once again, he thought it was Sunday and believed it was time to walk to church in order to preach. It seems there was always a sermon burning in his soul, ready to be preached.

Final Meeting with Colleagues (17 November 1572)

On Sunday, 16 November, Knox chose not to eat because he assumed it was a fast day. The following day, he requested that the leading members of St. Giles' come to his house. On that Monday, 17 November, one week before Knox would die, he met with his ministerial colleagues in Edinburgh to leave them with his final charge. Gathered at his bedside was his successor, James Lawson, along with the elders and deacons of St. Giles' and David Lindsay, one of the ministers of Leith. Knox addressed this group with the following words:

> The day now approaches and is before the door ... And now my God is my witness, whom I have served in the Spirit, in the gospel of his Son, that I have taught nothing but the true and solid doctrine of the gospel of the Son of God ... that if it were possible I might gain them to the Lord. But a certain reverential fear of my God, who called me and was pleased of his grace to make me a steward of divine mysteries to whom I knew I must render an account when I shall appear before his tribunal of the manner in which I have discharged the embassy which he hath committed unto me, had such a powerful effect as to make me utter so intrepidly whatever the Lord put into my mouth without respect of persons. [8]

8   Knox, *The Works of John Knox, Vol. 6*, p. 655.

On 22 November, various members of the High Church visited Knox as he lay on his deathbed. After they left, the two ministers, Lawson and Lindsay, remained. His deathbed became a pulpit as he charged his successor:

> Fight the good fight, do the work of the Lord with courage and with a willing mind; and God from above bless you, and the church whereof you have the charge, against which the gates of hell shall not prevail.[9]

On His Deathbed (24 November 1572)

On 24 November, as Knox lay in bed, a friend asked if he had any pain. Knox replied, 'It is no painful pain, but such a pain as shall soon, I trust, put an end to the battle.'[10] Knox then asked his wife to read to him again Scripture and sermons. At midday, she repeatedly read to him 1 Corinthians 15. 'Is not that a comfortable chapter,'[11] he said, clinging to the promise of the gospel and the hope of the resurrection. He then pointed with three fingers upward to heaven and said, 'I commend my soul and spirit and body unto thy hands, O Lord.'[12] After another five hours, Knox instructed his wife, 'Go read where I have cast my first anchor,'[13] a reference to John 17. Finally, she once more read to him a part of Calvin's sermons on Ephesians.

Knox lay quiet on his deathbed for some hours. Then, at eleven o'clock that night, Knox sighed, 'Now it is come.'[14] Bannatyne encouraged him to think on the Lord Jesus Christ

---

9   Knox, *The Works of John Knox, Vol. 6*, p. 656.

10   Ibid., p. 643.

11   Ibid.

12   Ibid.

13   Ibid.

14   Ibid.

and His promises. Knox lay speechless; there was no verbal response. His loyal secretary asked for a sign that he could still hear. Knox raised up one of his hands to heaven. He then died peacefully.

In the words of his secretary, Richard Bannatyne:

> In this manner departed this man of God: the light of Scotland, the comfort of the church within the same, the mirror of godliness, and pattern and example of all true ministers.[15]

Buried at St. Giles' (26 November 1572)

Two days later, the funeral of the leader of the Scottish Reformation was held at St. Giles'. The service was followed by Knox's burial in the churchyard. A large crowd assembled, including the aristocracy of the city. At his funeral, Earl Morton, the newly elected Regent of Scotland, spoke these long-remembered words: 'Here lies a man who in his life never feared the face of man.'[16] In a sad irony of history, his burial place is presently beneath the parking lot next to the church, in space number 23.

A reflection upon the prolific life of Knox reveals that he was the founding architect of the Church of Scotland. He gave this influential nation deep roots in Reformed theology and Presbyterianism. Further, he planted the seeds for the later development of Covenant thought in

---

15 Richard Bannatyne, as quoted by Iain H. Murray in *John Knox and the Reformation* (Edinburgh: Banner of Truth, 2011), p. 130.

16 Knox, *The Works of John Knox, Vol. 6*, p. liii.

Scotland, laying the groundwork for the Covenanters movement in the seventeenth century. Believers down through the centuries, not only in Scotland, but around the world, especially in England and the United States, stand on the broad shoulders of Knox and follow the path he marked. Knox had become, as Martyn Lloyd-Jones described him, 'the founder of Puritanism,'[17] the powerful movement within the Church of England that attempted to 'purify' it according to Protestant principles shortly after the ascension of Elizabeth I of England in 1558.

The church today owes an enormous debt to the stand taken by Knox 500 years ago. Far-reaching movements that impact large swaths of people often begin with just one person. At the center of the Scottish Reformation was an emboldened individual who knew his God and knew God's Word. Chiseled onto the Reformation Wall in Geneva next to Knox are his words: '*Un homme avec Dieu est toujours dans la majorité.*' He became the embodiment of these words, which mean:

'One man with God is always in the majority.'

---

17   Lloyd-Jones, 'John Knox—The Founder of Puritanism,' *The Puritans: Their Origins and Successors*, p. 260.

NINE

Enduring Legacy

(c. 1514–72)

Reaching down through the centuries and extending to this present hour, the legacy of John Knox remains firmly implanted in many areas of the worldwide church. Knox was influential in the formation of a Reformed church government and polity, education, and doctrinal creed. However, the one area in which Knox proved to be most impactful was in a return to biblical preaching. Every history-altering reformation begins at this point. The Reformers were first and foremost preachers. To understand the force of their lives is to grasp the impact of their pulpit ministries. J. H. Merle d'Aubigne, the noted historian of the Reformation in Europe, has written, 'The only true Reformation is that which emanates from the Word of God.'[1] This is especially true with Knox in Scotland.

---

1   J. H. Merle d'Aubigne, *The Reformation in England, Vol. 1 Book 2*, edited by S. M. Houghton (1853, repr.; Edinburgh: Banner of Truth, 1994), p.143.

A man known for his biblical preaching, Knox has been called 'the greatest of Scotsmen.'[2] Through his expositions of Scripture, he established Scotland as a fortress for Reformed truth. He was 'the Reformer of his country,'[3] who ushered in the Scottish Reformation, principally, through his pulpit power. The recovery of biblical preaching found its champion in this emboldened figure.

Throughout his ministry, Knox remained focused upon the preaching of the Word. While in England, he was a pastor and then an itinerant preacher, proclaiming the Word throughout the country. While in Europe, he pastored and preached in both Frankfurt and Geneva. During his time in Edinburgh, Knox preached to his congregation at St. Giles' twice on the Lord's Day and three times during the week. In addition, he conducted extensive preaching tours throughout the country. Whether in his own pulpit or traveling, whether in a church building or private home, Knox was incessantly preaching wherever he was.

As a powerful and prolific preacher of the Word, the influence of Knox on preaching in Scotland was staggering. In 1560, when Knox returned to his homeland, there were only twelve ministers in the whole of Scotland. Seven years later, there were 250 ministers. In addition, there were 150 'exhorters' and 450 lay leaders who ministered the Scriptures. The bold preaching of Knox inspired the preaching of other courageous men, and the pulpit ministry of this valiant Reformer filled Scotland with a love for preaching God's Word. Noted historian of preaching John Broadus recounts

---

2   James Stalker, *John Knox: His Ideas and Ideals* (London: Hodder and Stoughton, 1904), p. 4.

3   Thomas Thompson, 'John Knox and His Writings,' *Select Practical Writings of John Knox* (1845, repr.; Edinburgh: Banner of Truth, 2011), p. xiii.

standing in Knox's pulpit in Stirling some three centuries later and longing to catch something of Knox's 'bold and zealous spirit'[4] in preaching.

The strong character of John Knox's ministry of the Word resonates across the centuries. The commitments described below are worthy guideposts for later generations of preachers as well.

A High View of Divine Calling

First, Knox believed he had been personally called by God to preach the Word. The pulpit was not a domain he had entered by his own initiative. Rather, he was convinced that this was a sacred station to which God had sovereignly appointed him. When first urged to take up the work of preaching, Knox burst into tears and refused. He stated that he would not run where God had not called him. Only when assured that God had chosen him for this high calling would he proceed. Reflecting upon this divine summons, Knox stated:

> Considering myself called of my God to instruct the ignorant, comfort the sorrowful, confirm the weak, and rebuke the proud; by tongue and lively voice in these corrupt days rather than to compose books for the age to come, seeing that so much is written, and yet so little well observed, I decree to contain myself within the bounds of that vocation whereunto I found myself especially called.[5]

The inward persuasion of such a high calling was necessary if Knox was to remain steadfast in his preaching in the difficult

---

4   John A. Broadus, *Lectures on the History of Preaching* (Birmingham, AL: Solid Ground Christian Books, 2004), p. 196.

5   Knox, *The Works of John Knox, Vol. 6*, p. lxxxvi.

days that lay ahead. He must *know* God had called him to this demanding office. Otherwise, he would flee in difficult times. He said: 'It hath pleased God, of his superabundant grace, to make me and appoint me, most wretched of many thousands, a witness, minister, and preacher.'[6] Knox considered himself unworthy of such an exalted position and calling. This, however, proved to aid in his reliance upon God for every syllable he uttered. He prayed, 'O Lord eternal, move and govern my tongue to speak the verity.'[7]

A High View of God's Word

Second, Knox believed that the Bible is the infallible Word of the living God. He possessed an unshakable confidence in the divine authorship and supernatural character of the sacred Scripture. He wrote, 'The person of the speaker is wretched, miserable, and nothing to be regarded, but things that were spoken are the infallible and eternal truth of God.'[8] Knox saw himself as mere clay within the hands of the Potter. It was not his own self-derived message that shook a nation, but the 'infallible and eternal truth of God.'

Knox was convinced that when the Bible speaks, God speaks. This was Knox's unwavering conviction:

> For as the Word of God is the beginning of life spiritual, without which all flesh is dead in God's presence, and the lantern to our feet, without the brightness whereof all the posterity of Adam doth walk in darkness, and as it is the foundation of faith, without which no man understandeth the good will of God, so it is also the only organ and instrument which God uses to strengthen the weak, to

6   Knox, *The Works of John Knox, Vol. 4*, p. 467.

7   Ibid., *Vol. 3*, p. 33.

8   Ibid., *Vol. 4*, p. 105.

comfort the afflicted, to reduce to mercy by repentance such as have slidden, and finally to preserve and keep the very life of the soul in all assaults and temptations, and therefore if that you desire your knowledge to be increased, your faith to be confirmed, your consciences to be quieted and comforted, and finally your soul to be preserved in life, let your exercise be frequent in the law of your God.[9]

Consequently, when Knox preached the Bible, he was persuaded God was speaking through him. A naturally timid man, his reclusive nature vanished when he mounted the pulpit and opened God's Word. He knew he was a mere messenger of the divine message power that brought life to the spiritually dead and strength to the weak.

A High View of Fearing God

Third, Knox was profoundly aware that on the last day, he must give an account of himself as a preacher to the One who had called him into the ministry. This sobering reality filled him with reverential awe for God and made him unshakable before men and women. Because Knox feared God, he did not fear humans. He preached so strongly because he feared God so deeply. Consequently, when he stood in the pulpit, he roared like a lion. Knox confided:

Whatever influenced me to utter whatever the Lord put into my mouth so boldly, and without respect of persons, was a reverential fear of my God, who called and of his grace appointed me to be *a steward of divine mysteries*, and a belief that he will demand an account of the manner in which I have discharged *the trust committed to me*, when I shall stand at last before his tribunal.[10]

---

9   Knox, *Works of John Knox*, *Vol. 4*, p. 133.

10 Thomas M'Crie, *The Life of John Knox* (1811, repr.; Glasgow: Free Presbyterian Publications, 1960), p. 196.

Knox was gripped with 'a certain reverential fear of my God, who called me.'[11] It would be before God 'I knew I must render an account when I shall appear before his tribunal.'[12] Knox preached with this constant reality in view. In the future, he would stand before God as a steward and answer for the ministry and message entrusted to him. Such final reckoning before God gripped his soul and kept a healthy reverence within him.

A High View of Diligent Study

Fourth, Knox was gifted with a brilliant mind, which he devoted to the diligent study of Scripture. Regarded for 'his proficiency as a scholar,'[13] he believed preaching the Word demanded his best mental preparation. Consequently, he was habitually absorbed in the disciplined reading of the Bible and in digging into commentaries. William Taylor records the widespread understanding that Knox's careful study of the Scripture made him so powerful in the pulpit:

> It was his habit to speak from a few notes which were made on the margin of his Bible, and which remained the sole written memoranda of his discourse ... Yet [his sermons] were as carefully premeditated as if they had been written ... He prepared with care ... and remembered with accuracy. He did not speak extemporaneously, in the sense of never having thought upon his subject until he was required to speak, but he had fixed beforehand his line of thought, and there is reason to believe also, in many cases, the very words in which he had determined to express himself. Yet,

11   Knox, *The Works of John Knox, Vol. 6*, p. 655.

12   Ibid.

13   Thomas Thompson, 'John Knox and His Writings,' *Select Practical Writings of John Knox*, p. xiii.

though he premeditated very carefully, he was able also to introduce what was given to him at the moment.[14]

In his preparation for preaching, Knox drew on his knowledge of the biblical languages. Broadus points out:

> Knox is a notable example of entering upon the ministry late in life. Educated for the Catholic priesthood, but early deposed because of Protestant heresy, he meant to spend his time as professor and public lecturer, but was pressed into the ministry at the age of forty-two ... About this time he learned Greek, and at the age of forty-nine we find him at Geneva, busily studying Hebrew.[15]

In addition, Knox read both ancient and modern theological writers and used the best commentaries available to him. In one of his letters, Knox described himself as 'sitting at my books'[16] and contemplating Matthew's Gospel by the help of 'some most godly expositions, and among the rest Chrysostom.'[17] Though a decisive man of action, he was also a diligent student who sat before his books in order to gain a deeper understanding of the truth.

A High View of Sequential Exposition

Fifth, Knox often preached through entire books of the Bible, or at least through extended sections of them. Knox desired to expound the biblical text phrase by phrase, finding clarity via 'an appeal from a difficult passage to a plainer,

---

14 William M. Taylor, *The Scottish Pulpit: From the Reformation to the Present Day*, pp. 46-7.

15 Broadus, *Lectures on the History of Preaching*, p. 195.

16 Knox, *The Works of John Knox, Vol. 3*, p. 350.

17 Ibid.

clearer passage in Scripture itself.'[18] When he first expounded Scripture in St. Andrews, he taught his pupils and interested hearers by proceeding through the Gospel of John. At other times, he worked his way through the books of the Old Testament prophets such as Isaiah, Daniel, or Haggai. As the lead author of *The First Book of Discipline,* Knox wrote that preaching should be according to 'the plain reading or interpretation of the Scripture.'[19] This approach necessitates that the duty of preaching be carried out with considerable care given to the authorial intent, historical context, and specific theme of the biblical book. Knox stated:

> By frequent reading, this gross ignorance, which in this cursed Papistry has overflowed all, may partly be removed. We think it most expedient that the Scripture be read in order, that is, that some one book of the Old or New Testament be begun and orderly read to the end. And the same we judge of preaching where the minister for the most part remains in one place. Skipping and deviating from place to place in Scripture, be it in reading or be it in preaching, we judge not so profitable to edify the Church, as the continual following of one text.[20]

In other words, Knox believed that a preacher should start with a text of Scripture and stay with it to the end, addressing each section of the book in turn without skipping from one section to the next. When preaching, he would normally spend half an hour calmly explaining the text before thundering out the application and exhortation to his

---

18   John Knox quoted by J. H. S. Burleigh, *A Church History of Scotland* (London: Oxford University Press, 1960), p. 157.

19   Knox, *The Works of John Knox, Vol. 2*, p. 239.

20   Ibid.

hearers. With unreserved diligence, Knox was dedicated to the exposition of Scripture.

A High View of Reformed Theology

Sixth, Knox was firmly committed in his preaching to the sound doctrine of the Reformers. This was the result of his thorough study of Scripture as well as his close associations with such notable Reformed leaders as George Wishart, John Calvin, Theodore Beza, and others. From the beginning of his pulpit ministry, the doctrine of justification by faith alone was prominent in his sermons. He claimed *sole fide* was the axe he had laid to the root of the Roman tree to demolish it. In his *Epistle to His Brethren in Scotland,* Knox sums up his commitment to the material principle of the Reformation in the following words:

> If therefore the doctrine and persuasion of any man tend to the exaltation and advancement of any righteousness or perfection, except of Christ Jesus alone; if any affirm that Christian justice which is available before God by any other perfection than remission of our sins, which we have by only faith in Christ's blood, or if any promise such perfection in this life that unfeignedly we need not say, 'Remit to us our offences, for we are unprofitable servants,' and finally, if any persuade that our merits, good works or obedience be any cause either of our justification, or yet of our election, let him be accursed.[21]

No pulpit can be any stronger than the saving gospel it proclaims. Knox preached that the perfect righteousness of Jesus Christ is given freely to sinners by grace alone, through faith alone, in Christ alone. Only the blood of Christ, he declared, can

---

21   Knox, *Works of John Knox, Vol. 4*, p. 272.

take away sins. Any reliance upon good works instead of the finished work of Christ renders one accursed by God.

A High View of Divine Sovereignty

Seventh, Knox strongly asserted the absolute sovereignty of God over all things. This supreme authority, he proclaimed, extends to all matters of providence, salvation, and divine judgment. Knox was persuaded that if the church is to be strong, this truth of God's supreme authority must be preached. In the Preface to *Predestination*, Knox maintained that this foundational truth is necessary for true humility, transcendent worship, and strong faith:

> The doctrine of God's eternal predestination is so necessary to the church of God that, without the same, can faith neither be truly taught, neither surely established; man can never be brought to true humility and knowledge of himself, neither yet can he be ravished in admiration of God's eternal goodness, and so moved to praise him as appertaineth.[22]

On another occasion, Knox wrote of the uncontested sovereignty of God:

> For as our God in his own nature is immutable, so remaineth his love toward his elect always unchangeable (Eph. 1); for as in Christ he hath chosen his church before the beginning of all ages, so by him will he maintain and preserve the same unto the end.[23]

Knox's confidence that God was in absolute control of every aspect of human history underwrote his vehement courage and empowered him to speak the truth of Holy Scripture to queens, kings, noblemen, and commoners alike.

---

22   Knox, *The Works of John Knox, Vol. 5*, p. 25.

23   Ibid., *Vol. 6*, p. 267.

A High View of Exalting Christ

Eighth, Knox believed that the highest aim of preaching the Scripture must be the proclamation of Jesus Christ. He concluded that he 'labored with all [his] power to gain them to Christ.'[24] The Lord Himself must be magnified in all the matchless glory of His divine person, exalted offices, and saving work. This riveted focus upon Christ was a primary element of preaching for Knox:

> There is no other name by which men can be saved but that of Jesus, and that all reliance on the merits of others is vain and delusive; that the Saviour having by His own sacrifice sanctified and reconciled to God those who should inherit the promised kingdom. All other sacrifices which men pretend to offer for sin are blasphemous. All men ought to hate sin, which is so odious before God that no sacrifice but the death of His Son could satisfy for it. They ought to magnify their heavenly Father, who did not spare Him who is the substance of His glory, but gave Him up to suffer the ignominious death of the cross for us. Those who have been washed from their former sins are bound to lead a new life, fighting against the lusts of the flesh, and studying to glorify God by good works.[25]

Until the concluding days of his ministry, Knox maintained this singular focus upon preaching Christ.

A High View of Passionate Preaching

Ninth, Knox was known as a fiery preacher of the Word of God. Nowhere were his passions more ignited than when he stood in the pulpit before God's people with an open Bible. Knox was not merely orthodox in his preaching, though that was

---

24 Douglas Bond, *The Mighty Weakness of John Knox* (Orlando, FL: Reformation Trust, 2011), p. 51.

25 M'Crie, *The Life of John Knox*, p. 82.

certainly true; orthodoxy alone may have the form of godliness without its power. Instead, Knox's spiritual power in the pulpit lay in the dynamic manner with which he delivered his sound message. Knox was the leading example of the observation made by John Broadus, 'The Scotch preachers ... have as a rule been more fiery and impassioned than the English.'[26] Thomas Thompson notes, 'His zeal in the pursuit of truth, and boldness in proclaiming it ... were his great characteristics.'[27] None who heard Knox could dispute this claim.

In describing this passionate preaching of Knox, William Taylor further states:

> [The pulpit] was the [magnifying] glass which focused all his powers into a point and quickened them into an intensity which kindled everything it touched. It brightened his intellect, enlivened his imagination, clarified his judgment, inflamed his courage, and gave fiery energy to his utterances ... There, over and above the fervid animation which he had in such large measure, and the glow of enthusiasm which fills the soul of the orator as he addresses an audience, he had the feeling that he was called of God to be faithful, and that lifted him entirely out of himself. He spoke because he could not but speak, and his words went *in* to men; like these modern missiles which burst within the wounds which they have made, so his words *exploded within the hearts* of those who received them and set them on fire with convictions that flamed forth in conduct. It was apparently impossible for anyone to listen to him without being moved either to antagonism or to agreement, or—for he could be tender also—to tears.[28]

---

26 Broadus, *Lectures on the History of Preaching*, p. 196.

27 Thompson, 'John Knox and His Writings,' *Select Practical Writings of John Knox*, p. xiv.

28 Taylor, *The Scottish Pulpit: From the Reformation to the Present Day*, pp. 55-6.

Biographer Thomas M'Crie describes Knox's zeal in preaching this way:

> His ministerial functions were discharged with the greatest assiduity, fidelity and fervour. No avocation or infirmity prevented him from appearing in the pulpit. Preaching was the employment in which he delighted, and for which he was qualified by an extensive acquaintance with the Scriptures and by the happy art of applying them in the most striking manner to the existing circumstances of the Church and of his hearers. His powers of alarming the conscience and arousing the passions have been frequently celebrated, but he excelled also in unfolding the consolations of the gospel and in calming the breasts of those who were agitated by a sense of guilt or suffering under the ordinary afflictions of life. When he discoursed of the griefs and joys, the conflicts and triumphs, of genuine Christians, he described what he had himself known and felt.[29]

A High View of Intercessory Prayer

Tenth, Knox was a preacher who regularly petitioned God in prayer to bless the proclamation of His Word. He knew the success of his preaching ministry lay, ultimately, not with him, but with God. Knox was much *for* God because he was much *with* Him. He stood tall in the pulpit because he had kneeled low in prayer. The depth of his prayers determined the breadth of his preaching.

So powerful was Knox's prayer life that Charles H. Spurgeon once remarked, 'When John Knox went upstairs to plead (with God) for Scotland, it was the greatest event in Scottish history.'[30] Mary, Queen of Scots acknowledged the same: 'I am more afraid of [Knox's] prayers than an army of ten thousand men.'[31] After the death of King Edward VI, Knox wrote *A Treatise on Prayer*

---

29   M'Crie, *The Life of John Knox*, p. 208.

30   J. H. Merle d'Aubigne, *The Reformation in England, Vol. 1*, p. 18.

31   John Howie, *The Scots Worthies*, p. 57.

(1553) in which he exhorted the suffering believers in England to pray. Specifically, it was a charge to pray for the advancement of the gospel with the new monarch, Bloody Mary, upon the throne of England. Knox wrote:

> Where constant prayer is, there the petition is granted … The precept or commandment to pray is universal, frequently inculcated and repeated in God's scriptures. 'Ask, and it shall be given to you' (Matt. 7:7). 'Call upon me in the day of trouble' (Ps. 50:15). 'Watch and pray, that ye fall not into temptation' (Matt. 26:41). 'I command that ye pray ever without ceasing' (1 Thes. 5:17). 'Make deprecations incessantly, and give thanks in all things' (1 Tim. 2:1-2, 8) … He who, when necessity constrains, desires not support and help of God, does provoke his wrath no less than such as make false gods or openly deny God.[32]

It was this kind of fervent intercession that undergirded the faithful exposition of Knox's preaching.

> The empowered preaching of Knox is best summed up in what Thomas Randolph, the English ambassador, conveyed to William Cecil, the Secretary of State, in England in October 1561:
>
> I assure you, the voice of one man [Knox] is able in one hour to put more life in us than five hundred trumpets continually blustering in our ears.[33]

---

32 Knox, *Works of John Knox, Vol. 3*, p. 91.

33 Knox, *The History of The Reformation in Scotland*, quoting Randolph to Cecil, October 7, 1561, p. 283.

Such was the powerful effect of Knox's preaching. His one voice was louder and more compelling than an entire army of other men. His trumpet-like call rallied the church in Scotland, England, and Europe to the high cause of the Reformation. His proclamations of the Scripture were used by God to put grace into the heart of countless multitudes who heard him.

How could anyone be so bold and courageous as Knox? The answer lies not with Knox himself, but with the Holy Spirit who indwelt him. God the Spirit fueled the fire within him. Knox acknowledged this in countless ways, noting with humility,

> God gave His Holy Spirit to simple men in great abundance.[34]

---

34   John Knox quoted by Iain Murray, *David Martyn Lloyd-Jones: The Fight of Faith 1939-1981* (Edinburgh: Banner of Truth, 1990), p. 382. [Knox's *Works*, 1846, Vol. I, p. 101.]

Concluding Thoughts

The life of John Knox is an example for all who love God and desire to see His name exalted. The urgent need of this present hour is for John Knox's gospel to rumble in pulpits and resound throughout the church. Both preachers and laypeople alike can join Knox in the courageous, bold, and persistent proclamation of the truths of God's Word.

John Knox was a leader in his time. In this present hour, the church of God remains in dire need of such leaders who are firmly committed to the exclusivity and sufficiency of Scripture. If the kingdom of God is to advance, it will require fearless men like John Knox to step forward and blow their Master's trumpet.

To be sure, the preparation of such men always comes at a high price. As in the case of Knox, God may sovereignly use adversity and opposition as a means of refinement and preparation in the lives of His servants of the Word. With divine flame, He removes the impurities from men's lives so they can be mightily used in kingdom work.

God sovereignly gives to His church those who, in the face of much adversity, steadfastly persevere and valiantly lead His sheep to higher spiritual ground. In this demanding hour, there is a pressing need for such faithful servants, cut from the same cloth as Knox, to lead the charge to restore the authority of God's Word to the church. Such heroic men must fill the pulpit and speak the truth with equal boldness to that seen in Scotland in the sixteenth century.

May God give to His church again strong men possessed with the indomitable spirit of John Knox The gentle flute or plaintive violin have their place, but they will never awaken a slumbering church in this dark hour. Give us men with a trumpet to their lips, sounding their Master's message, plainly and boldly, to the ears of all.

If a new Reformation is to come, it will come through the Spirit-empowered preaching of the Word of God in pulpits around the world. May the example of Knox embolden preachers and all who know Christ to herald His saving gospel. May a new generation declare the truth of Scripture in the broadest context of the full counsel of God.